HISTORICAL

ATLAS OF

EUROPE

HISTORICAL ATLAS OF EUROPE

Ian Barnes
and
Robert Hudson

ARCADIA EDITIONS LIMITED

This edition first published in Great Britain in 1998 by
ARCADIA EDITIONS LIMITED,
Shirley,
Derbyshire,
England

A Simon and Schuster Macmillan Company
1638 Broadway, New York, N.Y. 10019-6785

A catalogue record of this book can be obtained from the British
Library.

ISBN 1-902305-00-0

FOREWORD

Europe has been forged through conquest, occupation and hegemony, while its peoples have shared and disputed a variety of philosophical, religious, economic and cultural beliefs, values and practices.

The History Atlas of Europe explores the extraordinary sweep of Europe's development, commencing with the origins of the earliest peoples and the classical past, through Christendom, to the balance of power politics of the seventeenth and eighteenth centuries, before concentrating on issues and developments in the nineteenth and twentieth centuries. The Atlas discusses aspects of art, culture, trade, thought and religion to provide a more rounded treatment than more conventional historical atlases. The spread of Celtic peoples through Europe is juxtaposed with the end of Greek Mediterranean hegemony through the Peloponnesian War and the rise of Rome on the Italian Peninsula, with its growth of empire and path of conquest. The gradual decline that set in after Diocletian's reforms at the end of the third century is followed by collapse from internal weakness in the face of Germanic invasions.

Since the time of Diocletian the empire had divided into two parts, and this cleavage would persist with the rise of the Byzantine empire in the East and the Frankish kingdoms in the West. East-West differences would deepen with the schism between Orthodox and Catholic variations of confession in 1054 and impact upon Europe yet again in the Early Modern period. The onset of new directions in faith, trade, politics and society would widen the rift even further. The effect of the Enlightenment, the ideas and ideals of the French Revolution and industrialization would widen and exacerbate this difference, in a process that has continued well into our own century.

One thing becomes clear throughout the progression of this work: that the constantly changing boundaries of Europe have expanded or contracted due to influences from beyond, with Europe as little more than a peninsula on the edge of Asia, spreading at its greatest extent from the Atlantic to the Urals and from the North Cape to the Mediterranean. This book therefore traces the thread of a common European identity based on common historical experiences in a celebration of diversity.

The origins of feudalism are illustrated by the map on Charlemagne and analyzed throughout the remainder of the section on "Christian Europe". Conflicts over religious differences are examined against the backdrop of the rise of the state and the growth of absolutism as a political formation and the balance of power through the wars of Louis XIV and the collapse of the Swedish empire.

One area which we considered most significant was revolution and the rise of nationalism. Here we found that changes in the nature of kingship in England, new political forms in the Dutch Republic, the impact and legacy of the French Revolution and state-building in Germany and Italy all had their specific roles to play. The Bolshevik Revolution — a critique in action of previous liberal and capitalist developments — seemed to provide a logical conclusion to this section.

The last two sections of the book locate Europe within the wider world and consider the rise and fall of European colonial empires and the impact of two major wars upon the European continent. As Europe enters the twenty-first century, two key issues, "deepening" and "widening", confront the European communities. To what extent will Europe progress down the road toward becoming a federal, supranational state; and how does Europe respond to the enormous changes that have taken place in eastern Europe since the fall of the Berlin Wall, the end of the Cold War and the break-up of the Soviet Union? Might the return to nationalism, irredentism and debates over sovereignty and self-determination result in further European discord?

In putting this book together, we both realize that some areas of European history have received less attention. This is both a reflection of our personal interests and editorial constraints.

Ian Barnes and Robert Hudson

CONTENTS

PART I: EARLIEST PEOPLES AND SETTLEMENTS

Myth, legend, and debate shroud the origins and history of Europe's early peoples and settlement. The first hominids travelled from Africa some million years ago, probably being related to *Homo erectus* and survived by hunting and gathering, working in harmony with the seasons. Early hominid archaeological finds are scattered throughout Europe, with the earliest sites situated around the Mediterranean. Northerly areas were only occupied during warmer periods in the Ice Ages. More evidence of hominid activity derives from discoveries like pebble tools, butchered animal bones and stone hand axes. These sites tend to follow river valleys as a means of penetrating new territories and to be by lakes, reliable supplies of water being essential for survival. Dwelling in cave communities or in huts at Bilzingsleben, these early man-ape peoples tamed fire and were capable of cooperation in big-game hunting, evidenced by elephant remains at Terralba-Ambrona in Spain. Large animals, including rhinoceros, were driven over cliffs, as seen at La Cotte de St. Brelade in the Channel Islands, although late Neanderthal man might have been responsible for this massacre.

The discovery of Neanderthal man in Germany in 1856 eventually sparked a controversy over the origins of early man. In 1921, a Neanderthal skull, differing slightly from the first, was found in Zambia and was classed as a new subspecies, Rhodesian man. In reality, Neanderthals varied as to climate, but the apparent minor differences led to theories of parallel development claiming that modern man evolved simultaneously, with Europeans from Neanderthals and Africans from Rhodesian man. Archaeology now suggests a widely held "Out of Africa" theory that Rhodesian man changed into *Homo sapiens* and broke out of sub-Saharan Africa to eventually populate Asia and Australia, and then entered Europe, gradually extinguishing the Neanderthal population. The Neanderthals are often stereotyped as primitive and brutish cavemen, but evidence suggests few differences between them and modern man; certainly their brains were equal in size. Living in social groups and using tools, particularly the Mousterian stone type, Neanderthals were dispersed from the Mediterranean to the glacial areas of northern Europe, and from Portugal to

Comparative skeletons of Neanderthal (right) and Cro Magnon (left). The Neanderthal shows a shorter, more powerful build, while Cro-Magnon, with a taller and lighter build — apart from the heavier brow ridge — could almost be a modern human.

central Asia, with heavy concentration of finds in the caves of southwestern France. That at La Ferrassie displayed a Neanderthal cemetery of two adults and three children. Elsewhere, in Iraq at Shanidar, a body was accompanied by flowers. Evidence therefore suggests that Neanderthals were strong, socially organized, adaptable to different environments and showed compassion in bur-

Stonehenge is perhaps one of the most famous pre-historic sites in the world. Its building began around 3100 BC and was then rearranged over a period of some 1200 years.
Its final form, seen today, dates from 1550 BC.
From the beginning the main axis of the structure has been aligned with the midsummer sunrise, and it is possible that the stones also align with other astronomical objects. The site allowed its builders to mark the changing seasons, as well as providing a focus for religious ceremony.

ial rites. The spread of hunter-gatherers into Europe generally followed river valleys, often along deer migration trails, movements often being dependent on fish supplies, especially salmon, an important dietary component. Technology developed apace, seeing the introduction of new stone flaking techniques, spear throwers, spears, harpoons, bows, fish hooks, and nets. Social organization and communal hunting methods grew throughout Europe, but cultural evolution became more specialized. Although the distribution of Venus figurines is widespread, suggesting some common cultural elements and contact, regional variations about stone tools might lead to speculation about regional identities and cultural differences.

The existence of Paleolithic Venus figurines points to an interest in art and maybe religion. Highly significant are the variety of cave paintings. The bas-relief painted Venus of Laussel in the French Dordogne is arguably an earth-mother goddess and pinnacle of a matriarchal society. Cave art was often carried out in inaccessible places, implemented by ladders and artificial light. The pictures at Altimira are particularly interesting, with an eighteen-metre-long painted ceiling of bison coexisting with many other animal representations, some now extinct. The Stone Age societies were superseded by Neolithic civilizations reaching the Atlantic coast by about 4000 BC (via the Danube and partly through the Mediterranean), bringing agriculture, stock-breeding and pottery. Accompanied by megalithic building, predominantly in the British Isles, France and Denmark, this civilization suddenly disappeared, possibly at the hands of invading battle-axe peoples entering from southern Russia and the Balkans; these groups introduced the Bronze Age, with its skilled metallurgy, spreading slowly from what are now the Czech and Slovak Republics to the Atlantic.

The first three recorded European civilizations thrived in the Bronze Age and were nurtured by Mediterranean trade. Minoan Crete was virtually an Aegean hegemonic power between 2200 and 1450 BC, succeeded by Mycenae on mainland Greece between 1450 and 1200 BC. In Italy, the Etruscans created western Europe's first civilization between 800 and 300. Each civilization made major contributions to trade, technology, art and religion. Crete also supplied the legend of the Minotaur, while Homer's *Iliad* and *Odyssey* brought the world classic verse and riddles for archaeologists yet to solve. Furthermore, historians have been introduced to "functional" history in Roman accounts of Etruscan life. Portrayed as vice-ridden and evil, Rome constantly sought to overshadow a civilization that had contributed so much to its own.

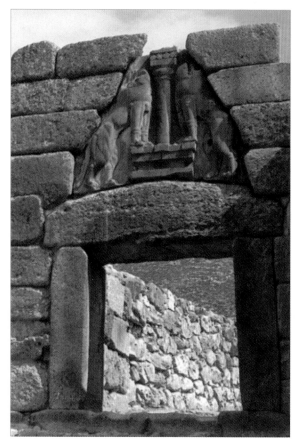

Aegean culture originally generated a Cycladic civilization, as seen in excavations made on Thera, Delos and surrounding islands. Pottery, jewellery and marble idols of human size have been unearthed, the latter being associated with the central fact of Cycladic life – the sea. Theran frescoes showed similarities with Minoan examples, but the island was destroyed by a volcanic eruption (c. 1625 BC). The islands exported obsidian, supported a fishing community and developed an important shipbuilding technology.

The Lion Gate at Mycenae, built around 1300 BC. So impressed were the ancient Greeks when they viewed the ruins they believed that the huge stones had been moved into position by a race of one-eyed giants, the "Cyclops".

Having ready access to quality timber, the Aegean peoples were constructing sail-driven boats, with keels, ribs and cutwaters. Evidence from a vase fragment found on the island of Syra, together with pictures on Cretan gems and seals, show ship development. After the fall of Knossos, some Minoans fled to Egypt, taking their skills with them and a ship model from the tomb at Medinet Haba near Luxor is reminiscent of Aegean craft.

In terms of trade, Crete and Mycenae were locked into an ever-increasing web of communications based upon mastery of the sea. The search for minerals was extremely important, since the civilizations were based on copper and tin, the former from Cyprus and the latter from Spain and maybe Cornwall in southwestern Britain. Pottery vessels containing perfumed oil were sent to Cyprus, Egypt, the Sudan, the Hittite empire in Anatolia, Sicily, Sardinia,

Malta and Etruria. In return, gold, ebony and ivory came from Egypt and Nubia, lapis lazuli from Afghanistan and amber from the Baltic. Knowledge of trade comes from both shipwrecks and grave finds. The existence of ritual burial with grave goods suggests a belief in an afterlife and religion. Lack of knowledge concerning Bronze Age religion prevents an accurate depiction of Cretan and Mycenaean cults. In the Cyclades, an open-air sanctuary with marble figurines was found on the island of Karos. The early period of Minoan culture likewise developed hilltop and mountain sanctuaries. The use of shrines seems prevalent, but little is known about the deities except that pictures of a goddess holding snakes are not uncommon. This snake deity's worship involved symbols of fertility and lunar and solar cycles. The major figure of reverence was a goddess or goddesses. Some clay figures were discovered at Ayia Irini in Ceos and at Mycenae. Many Mycenaean sites have terracotta figures with a woman's form. They possess beaklike noses and prominent breasts and might represent a fertility goddess. They wear flat headdresses and long skirts and appear to hold up their arms in an attitude of worship. Unlike Homer's Hades, Minoan Crete appeared to offer the dead the Isles of the Blessed.

The Minoan and Mycenaean architectural experiences are entirely different. The Minoan palaces were multifunctional, possessing spaces for worship, storage areas, workshops and living quarters. These were organized around a central courtyard and were totally unfortified. At Mycenae, Tiryns and Pylos, palaces tended to have a dominant central hall entered from a courtyard and were fortified with massive, irregular masonry blocks. Where painting but not sculpture are concerned, the Minoans outclassed Mycenae. Cretan murals depicted nature, animals and the notion of movement and their techniques and styles were exported to the Greek mainland. On Thera a recent excavation has uncovered one fresco representing the Aegean world with highly decorated ships sailing from port to port. Minoan sculpture includes bronze figurines in attitudes of worship and somersaulting bull-jumpers and statuettes incorporating and decorated with several different materials. The Cycladic civilization produced not just the life-sized painted women but many seated male figures playing harps or holding drinking cups. Mycenae produced geometric and figural commemorative plaques, some reliefs on the Lion Gate, ivory containers and statuettes. Both Minoan and Mycenaean pottery created pottery jars, mainly decorated with aspects of marine life such as octopus, cuttlefish and seaweed. Minoan pottery pictures tended to be free-flowing, while a more disciplined Mycenaean style introduced animal and human figures. Little Minoan metalwork survives, but Mycenaean craftsmanship is very impressive. Their shaft-graves produced Agamemnon's golden death mask, as well as gold and silver vases and ornamental bronze weapons inlayed with precious metals and sheathed in gold and ivory. Such beautiful items were prized all over the Aegean and a most memorable piece was the holed pomegranate pendant made by a Mycenaean jeweller around 1300 BC and found in Cyprus, a refuge for many

"In the ruins of Mycenae are the underground chambers of Atreus and his sons where they kept the treasure-houses of their wealth." *Pausanias*, The guide to Greece

This detail from a fresco in the Palace of Knossos dates from about 1600 BC and shows part of a procession of gift-bearers.

Greeks when the Mycenaean civilization eventually crumbled.

In contrast to the eastern Mediterranean, the western Etruscans have been overlooked by many historians. Whether sailing from Asia Minor or migrating from eastern Europe over the Alps, the Etruscans established (c. 800–400 BC) a confederation of twelve city-states in central Italy (modern Tuscany), gradually extending their control to the Po Valley and to the Adriatic at Spina and Adria and also to the bay of Naples, where they won control over Greek colonies, including Capua and Pompeii. They even turned the modest settlement of Rome into an Etruscan city ruled by the Tarquin kings. Eventually, the Gauls invaded the Po Valley, Campania fell to local Italic peoples, while Rome steadily acquired the rest of Etruria, crushing its culture and turning it into a Roman province. Originally each city was ruled by a king lording it over serfs and slaves. Wealth was based on iron ore extraction, Elban copper, cinnabar, tin, silver, lead and alum, used to fix pigments in cloth. Minerals were traded with Greeks and Phoenicians, and economic forces appear to be at the root of Etruscan internecine wars, alliances, and conflicts with Greeks and Romans. The author and poet D. H. Lawrence, in his poems "Cypresses", portrays the "long-nosed, sensitive-footed, subtly-smiling Etruscans" with their "fanciful long shoes" as being ephemeral, artistic and evasive, these views taken from Etruscan murals. Bright colours were used to depict vivacious games, dancing, music and banqueting. Women were shown sharing couches with men at mealtimes, riding in covered wagons to inspect estates and playing musical instruments at funerals, suggesting that aristocratic women were treated with more respect than their Roman and Greek counterparts, and that they achieved high social status and economic influence. In art, men are always engaged in activity; games, boar-hunting, processions, dances, banquets and diving. Toward the end of Etruscan civilization, murals became gloomy, portraying war scenes and demons after death, maybe instinctively depicting the inevitability of defeat at the hands of the dour Romans.

Etruscan tombs are witness to the power, wealth, and sophistication of their owners. Grave gifts provide microcosms of life through mirrors, bowls and other artifacts left with the dead. Frescoes such as that in a tomb at Chiusi picture hunting scenes, exotic birds and flowers, together with the journey to the afterlife. Religion took note of natural forces deified as gods of the sea, earth and rising sun. Greek gods and goddesses were renamed: Zeus, Hera and Athena became Tinia, Uni and Minerva; Vulcan, Bacchus and Mercury had counterparts. Catha was the sun god; Tiv, god of the moon; Thesan, god of the dawn; Turan was Venus and Applu, Apollo. Oriental and Greek symbols coexist; Egyptian sphinxes watch Etruscan winged demons charge dangerous Greek furies. Many elements of Etruscan religion were appropriated by the Romans. Other Etruscan influences on the Romans were considerable, giving them the toga, town planning, the villa and an alphabet only slightly modified. Etruria never died; it survived culturally.

An Etruscan bronze statuette of a warrior (originally he would also have been equipped with a shield and spear). Cast in bronze, it was found near Arezzo, Italy, and dates from around 550 BC.

13

HUMAN COLONIZATION

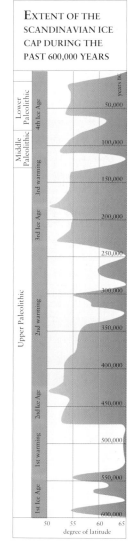

Many scientists assume that early hominids developed in southern Africa, but remains have been found in Tanzania, Kenya and southern Ethiopia. This *Australopithecus africanus* is associated with pebble tool industries; these crude tools were adequate enough for pounding plants and shredding meat. Some forms of these hominids are classified as *Homo habilis*, showing advanced tool skills; they may have hunted animals but more probably were vegetarians, supplementing their diet by scavenging carcasses. *Homo erectus* probably developed from this earlier hominid, as it is recognizably a human creature and capable of flaking stone to produce choppers. Evidence suggests that he was both a cave and river or lake bank dweller. Remains of *Homo erectus* at Vértesszölös near the Danube revealed stone implements and stone chips and what appears to be a hearth pointing to control of fire.

Homo erectus survived for some one and a half million years, probably thriving in the warm periods during the Ice Ages. By 250,000 years ago, new peoples were evolving and adapting to living in cold periods and about 150,000 years later, Neanderthal man emerged. He can be regarded as a separate species and lived during the last Ice Age in Eurasia. Remains from a number of sites have been found, noticeably in the Neander Valley, La Chapelle-aux-Saints, Le Moustier, La Ferrassie, La Quina, Gibraltar, Monte Circeo, Saccopastore, Ehringsdorf and Krapina, showing a geographic distribution in Germany, France, Spain, Italy and the Balkans. Were they a species adapted to the cold, a specialized offshoot from the human tree becoming extinct as the climate improved? Some Neanderthals are thought to have avoided cold-adaptation and developed into *Homo sapiens*. Another view places Neanderthals within human evolution and attributes their extinction to absorption into modern man, scattering a few genes in the process. Fossil finds show that Neanderthal tool kits, especially of the Mousterian culture, demonstrate spearmaking, a use of stone flakes and bone. They hunted large animals (elk), gathered nuts, roots, and tubers, had domesticated fire and could make huts constructed of animal skins on a frame of branches or mammoth bones.

When modern man emerged through natural selection, a process with huge gaps in the historical story, a variety of human types such as Cro-Magnon, Grimaldi and Brünn were capable of making flint-tipped spears and arrows, hunting in coordinated groups, developing bone tools (awls), flint drills, scrapers and cutters. Early man lived in caves, rock shelters and huts, developing an appreciation of decoration, sculpture and art. Engraved bone tools depicting a bison followed by a man were found at Laugierie Basse, France, while carved horses' heads on bone from Le Mas d'Azil show clear artistic appreciation. Venus figurines found all over Europe (Brno, Willendorf) show faceless, large-breasted, wide-hipped pregnant women and are assumed to be a fertility symbol. Painting using mineral colours was fairly widespread, communicating views about wildlife, hunting and perhaps even tradition and ritual. The techniques used were often sophisticated, using cave wall surfaces to achieve a three-dimensional effect.

EARLIEST PEOPLE AND SETTLEMENT

ice cover

☐ ice cover, c. 300000–200000 BC

▨ ice cover, c. 110000–15000 BC

sites

● Australopithecus advanced

◉ classical Neanderthal man

○ modern man of the late Upper Pleistocene

● site important both before and after
the climatic change of c. 10000 BC

Norwegian Sea

North Sea

Baltic Sea

Oban ●

Mulierup ●

Star Carr ●

Paviland ○   ● Bilzingsleben

Swanscombe ○   ◉ Neanderthal
            Engis ○ ◉ Obercassel
            Spy ○   ○ Ehringsdorf

St Brelade's Bay ○   Brünn ○   ○ Predmosti

River Rhine

ATLANTIC OCEAN   *River Loire*   Mauer ●   Ganovce ○   ● Vestonice   ● Szeleta
                                    ○ Steinheim   ● Vertesszöllös

Angles sur l'Anglin ●   Lascaux ●
La Madeleine ●   ○ Solutré Pouilly
Abri Suard ○ ● La Quina   ● La Chapelle aux Saints
Fontéchevade ○
Combe Capelle ○ ○ Chancelade
Laugerie Basse ○ ○ Le Moustier
Sauveterre la Lemance ●
        Cro-Magnon ○   ○ La Ferrassie

Altamira ●   Arago ○   Grimaldi ●
    Montmaurin ○
Tuc d'Audoubert ● Niaux ● ○ Lazaret
    Le Mas d'Azil ● ● La Porte

Corsica

Saccopastore ○
    Monte Circeo ○

Petralona ●

Sardinia

Adriatic Sea

River Danube

Aegean Sea

Balearic Is.

Forbes Quarry ●

Mediterranean Sea   *Sicily*

Ternifine ●

Arctic Circle

N

0   200 km

0   200 miles

15

FIRST FARMERS, 6500 BC

A shepherd tends his flock in the Provence region of southern France. In many areas across Europe the keeping of livestock has changed little, and traditional methods still exist, handed down from earliest times.

Agriculture and cattle farming reached the Aegean about 6500 BC but took another 2,000 to 3,000 years to spread throughout the temperate regions of Europe. Neolithic farming villages allowed the population to rapidly increase and to push settlements farther north and west. Settlements spread up the River Vardar to the north Balkans and into the lower Danubian Basin, complete with their common Starcevo-Körös style of painted and impressed-ware pottery. Villages made of mud-brick buildings were sometimes continuously occupied for hundreds of years, steadily accumulating debris until the village ended on a mound. This *tell* style of settlement is best exemplified by Karanovo in Bulgaria. The next phase of expansion saw movement through middle Europe into the Rhineland, the Low Countries and northern France in the west; into north Germany and Silesia in the north; and east into the Ukraine. The settlements comprised groups of rectangular wooden farmhouses surrounded by walls and ditches, but the population was still mobile. Slash-and-burn agricultural techniques meant a move every few seasons after soil exhaustion set in. Rested land would be reoccupied later. Gradually, Neolithic culture split into separate but overlapping cultures defined by their pottery styles. The Boian settlements developed in Romania and in the Tripolye around the Bug and Dnieper, while the funnel-necked beaker culture and the battle-axe culture lasted into the second millennium.

The movement from loess soil settlements along river valleys and plains to heavier, less productive ones made ploughing essential. The felling of forest land necessitated large supplies of flints and flint factories were established. Neoloithic mobility was aided by travel on rivers in dugout canoes and skin-covered boats and on land by sledges in snow, on oxen or reindeer-drawn wagons, later pulled by horses, and by building trackways of logs and branches in wetlands. Trade was extensive in grinding stones, knapped flints and amber and followed a variety of routes, along the Rhine, Elbe, Rhône, and Danube. Neolithic ingenuity is further evidenced by the construction of standing stones (menhirs) and various stone alignments (megaliths), the most famous being at Carnac in Brittany and Stonehenge in England. Dependence on stone tools gradually diminished as copper was mined by the different groups in central, northern and eastern Europe. These people produced knives, daggers and pins. Eventually, the mixture of tin and copper produced bronze, a harder metal. A variety of important Bronze Age cultures emerged; the Unetice culture of the Early Bronze Age was established in central Germany, Bohemia and Lower Austria, linking with Bell-beaker groups in Bavaria. The area was an important transit region for trade between the north and the Mediterranean. The Urnfield culture spread after 1300 BC, practicing cremation of the dead and the burial of ashes in urns. Sites have been found from Spain to eastern Europe, in Italy, southern Scandinavia and Britain. The degree of specialization involved in mining and smelting bronze would suggest that society was becoming differentiated, with tradesmen coexisting with farmers. Grave finds containing bronze swords would suggest the growth of a warrior caste.

SPREAD OF AGRICULTURE,
7000 BC–2000 BC

- 7000 BC
- 6000 BC
- 5000 BC
- 4000 BC
- 3000 BC
- 2000 BC

→ direction of spread

metal working

- early Copper Age
- late Copper Age
- early Bronze Age

▲ main source of tin in second milennium

MINOAN CRETE

A pouring vessel (rhyton) carved from serpentine in the form of a bull's head, from the Palace of Knossos.

Minoan culture was one of the three main cultures of Aegean civilization, the other two being the Cycladic and Mycenaean. This Bronze Age civilization has been associated in myth with Theseus and the Minotaur, but archaeological discoveries by Sir Arthur Evans in 1900 unearthed an example of a flourishing palace culture at Knossos, other buildings being found at Phaestos, Mallia and Zakros. The kings of Knossos achieved their greatest power between 2200 and 1450 BC, when they influenced the whole Aegean, trading widely with Egypt, Sicily, Cyprus and Syria while building colonies at Kastri on Cythera, on Rhodes and Miletus in Anatolia. Cretans also lived in towns such as Phylakopi on Melos and Agia Irini on Ceos. Copies of Cretan frescoes and motifs have been discovered in Tell-el-Daba in Egypt. Moreover, the bull-jumping scenes associated with Minoan bull sports were painted with Cretan, not Egyptian, colours.

The Cretan thalassocracy survived several rebuildings of its palaces following natural disasters and developed a brilliant culture that might have been cross-fertilized by mainland refugees from the Near East. So successful were the Minoans that letters found in Mari on the Euphrates attest to the quality of Cretan craftsmanship. Exports included woven wool textiles, pottery, metal vases, daggers, stone lamps and vases and timber products; imports included copper, scarab seals, iron, precious stones and ostrich eggs.

The most significant monument of Minoan history must be the Knossos palace. Rooms, on up to four levels, surrounded a central courtyard, demonstrating architectural sophistication best observed in the distinctive, downward-tapering Minoan columns and walls made of doors, allowing privacy and ventilation. The palace walls were often richly decorated with frescoes depicting landscapes and seascapes vitalized by animals, birds and foliage. Minoan artists excelled in carving marble figures, creating bronze figurines of bull-jumpers, replicating scenes on Knossos murals.

Cretan religion is portrayed by the sanctuaries within the palace at Knossos, associated with worship of a mother-goddess, possibly Rhea, and linked to pictures of a double axe appearing on the palace walls. A snake goddess also appears to be a figure of veneration, and the sympathetic portrayal of nature in the arts suggests a form of nature worship.

The collapse of Minoan culture coincided with the growth of the Mycenaean civilization in Greece, suggesting that this culture eclipsed and destroyed the Minoan cultural age.

Arkoudiotissa
Akrotiri
Kydonia ● Khania
Aptera

C

R

24°

MINOAN CRETE, c. 1500–1250 BC

■	palace		
▣	lesser palace or villa	⚓ port	
⌢	Tholos tomb	●	finds of Linear A text
◭	sacred cave	●	finds of Linear B text
▲	peak sanctuary	○	places mentioned in linear B text

royal road
or
"sacred way"
theatre

northeast house

pillar hall

north entrance

west court

storage rooms

throne room

main staircase
to first floor

central palace sanctuary

pillar crypts

altars

grand staircase

central court

royal apartments

Hall of the
Double Axes

staircase to
upper floor

covered stairway
to south entrance

south propylaeum

south
house

southeast
house

0   25 m

0   25 yds

N

THE PALACE OF KNOSSOS

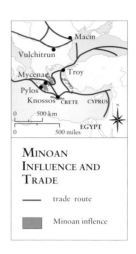

Macin

Vulchitrun

Mycenae   Troy

Pylos

Knossos   CRETE   CYPRUS

EGYPT

0   500 km

0   500 miles

N

MINOAN
INFLUENCE AND
TRADE

———   trade route

Minoan inflence

N

Dia

Dia

Cave of
Eileithyia

Katsambas

Pyrgos

Armenoi

Gonies   Giofyrakia

Knossos

Gypsades   Skoteino   Mallia

E

Idaean Cave

Sybrita   Tylissos

Juktas

Lyttos

Monastiraki

Apodhoulou   T   Archanes

Vathypetro   E

Karphi   Lato

Priniatiko

Dictaean   Pyrgos

Vasiliki

Kamares Cave

Yianisadhes

Itanos

Mochlos   Palaikastro

Pseira   Setaia

Myrsini   Menares

Zou

Prinias

Zakro

Gournia

Etiani

Triada

Paximadhia   Phaistos

Mitropolis   Viannos   Pyrgos   Myrtos

Kamilari   Platanos

Kommos   Porti   Koumasa

Kephali   Papoura   Kophinas   Inatos

Gaidhouronisi

Kouphonisi

Kouphonisi

0   10 km

0   10 miles

2,000

1,000

200

0 m

35°

25°

26°

19

MYCENAEAN GREECE

Mycenae, on the plain of Argolis, gave its name to a culture developed on mainland Greece during the late phase of the Bronze Age. Other major centres of Mycenaean culture included Tiryns, Pylos, Thebes and Argos. Mycenae, reputably the city of Agamemnon in the Homeric epics, was one of a series of heavily fortified strongholds built in a palatial style, following the example of Knossos. These edifices served as the military headquarters and administrative centres for the surrounding countryside.

Mycenae was the most powerful of the mainland Greek states between 1450 and 1200 BC. Shaft-grave finds including Linear B early Greek inscriptions have been found at numerous sites together with pottery, considerable quantities of weapons and armour, and funeral masks in beaten gold.

The German archaeologist Heinrich Schliemann uncovered Mycenae, with its massive cyclopean walls (1876–1878), its famous Lion Gate and the beehive tombs known as the Treasury of Atreus and the Tomb of Clytemnestra. His discoveries confirmed Homer's description of Mycenae as being "rich in gold". Grave finds include amber, ivory, ostrich egg beakers, gold and silver vases, amethysts and other objects demonstrating the extensive trade routes used and how Mycenaean culture was a fitting heir to Minoan Crete. Indeed, the palaces were similar to those in Crete, particularly in the utilization of frescoes, bathrooms and storage rooms. However, the more sophisticated Cretan style gave way to massive stone constructions demonstrated in the Lion Gate, but serving a similar function as storage and status centres.

A golden burial mask from a tomb at Mycenae, excavated by Heinrich Schliemann, so excited by this find he wrote:"I have looked upon the face of Agamemnon".

The power and influence of Mycenae was considerable if not dominant in the Aegean, where its sea power colonized the Cyclades, Crete, Cyprus, the Dodecanese, northern Greece, Macedonia and western Anatolia. Trade spread to Sardinia and southern Italy, as well as former Cretan markets. Mycenaean pottery has been found as far afield as Sudan and western Asia.

The art and architecture of Mycenae is reminiscent of Minoan Crete. Minoan artists carried their crafts to the mainland, as evidenced in the change of Mycenaean royal graves from shaft-graves to the Minoan tholos tomb, sometimes vaulted with thick stone roofs before being covered with earth tumuli.

The facade of one, named the Treasury of Atreus, is decorated with contrasting green and red marbles in the form of columns. Art flourished in the adornment of pottery, closely following Minoan themes, such as an octopus-painted jar found in a cemetery at a Mycenaean colony on Rhodes and a cuttlefish-decorated cup.

In 1900, a British archaeologist, Sir Arthur Evans, found baked clay tablets at Knossos dating from the middle of the second millennium BC, with two types of writing on them. These are called Linear A and Linear B; the former, the written language of Minoan Crete, has yet to be deciphered but the latter is an early form of Greek. The discovery of Linear B on Crete supports one historical explanation that Mycenaeans gained ascendancy over the Minoans.

Mycenae was destroyed about 1100 BC by fire. Historians cannot yet agree why this should have occurred, nor can they satisfactorily explain the collapse of Mycenaean civilization. Invasions by Dorians from the north might have caused this destruction, but equally famine or sea raiders might explain its demise.

TIRYNS CITADEL

— old citadel, 1400 BC

1. main gateway
2. inner gateway to palace
3. greater propælum
4. lesser propælum
5. court to chief Megaron
6. chief Megaron
7. court to lesser Megaron
8. lesser Megaron

MYCENAEAN GREECE

■ Mycenaean capital

• major city

• Mycenaean site

21

EARLY GREECE

.......At the end of the Bronze Age, waves of invaders (c. 1200–1000 BC) sifted down into ancient Greece, subjugating the indigenous peoples. These invaders, perhaps set in motion by Illyrian pressure, were militarily superior, using mounted warriors with iron weapons against the more primitively armed bronze weapons of the attacked. Some northwestern Greeks settled in Epirus, Aetolia and Acarnania, but the Dorians reached into the Peloponnesus by land and to Crete, the Dodecanese and southwest Anatolia by sea. Attica, Euboea and the Cyclades, inhabited by Ionians, either remained untouched by the Dorians or repelled them, and eventually settled Chios and the western coast of Anatolia. The Aeolians, from Thessaly, occupied Lesbos and areas farther north in Anatolia. Historians have debated the nature and timing of the Dorian invasions, but whatever theories are proffered, there is no denying that large-scale population movements occurred, and many Bronze Age sites were destroyed by fire (Mycenae, Tiryns, Pylos), setting in motion two centuries of chaos, after which the distribution of peoples is reflected by the disposition of the most important dialects. At the end of the Dark Ages, the Greeks spread throughout the Mediterranean, trade being a prime motive. The Greeks were therefore in a position to transmit aspects of advanced cultures from the Near East to western Europe. Many of the colonies became extremely rich. Legend has it that the people of Sybaris in southern

Achilles, the heroic ideal, admired by the Greeks, portrayed here on a vase of the 5th century BC.

Italy slept on beds of rose petals and roosters were banned from the town, lest the inhabitants would be woken up too early by raucous crowing. Eastern trade with Egypt and Syria became very important for Corinth, Rhodes and Ephesus.

The geography of Greece informs its political development. Living on islands, on promontories, in valleys separated by mountains on the mainland, people in small areas inaccessible from other parts developed a series of independent communities competing for the best land and creating a miscellaneous collection of city-states. Each state possessed a strong identity and citizens were extremely loyal to that home state and its patron deity. Despite their individuality, the city-states did sometimes league together against common enemies.

The city-states gradually produced a new property-owning noble class, developing aristocratic rule. Other forms of politics included oligarchies and despotic tyranny, but some states eventually created early forms of democracy. Athens provided an assembly where ordinary citizens, rich or poor, could speak and vote, making important decisions such as declaring war. In religion, the Greeks made use of shrines and temples, with a pantheon of deities each possessing their own spheres of influence: Apollo was associated with healing and medicine, while Athena was the goddess of wisdom and warfare and presided over literature, the arts and philosophy. This latter "love of wisdom" involved science, mathematics and political ideas. Heraclitus created an atomic theory, while Pythagoras developed theorems. Associated with philosophy are political thinkers who gradually reformed society. Leading figures are Solon, who outlawed debt slavery and Cleisthones, who developed equality of political rights, strongly influencing many modern democratic systems.

EARLY GREECE

Greek dialects and their expansion

Northwest   Arcadian

Aeolic   Dorian

Ionian

ETRUSCAN EXPANSION

A detail from "Tomb of the Leopards" showing musicians at an Etruscan funerary banquet, 6th century BC.

The Etruscans, a people allegedly from southwestern Asia Minor, Lydia according to Herodotus, built the first civilization of western Europe from the eighth to third centuries BC in central Italy, in a region known as Etruria, modern-day Tuscany. Subjugating the mineral-wealthy region between the Arno and Tiber, an Etruscan nobility founded a loosely knit League of Twelve Cities, probably dominating the local population. Some major cities were at Veii, Tarquinii, Vulci, Volaterrae and Visentium. Their power expanded by colonization to the north into the Po Valley and to the south beyond Rome into the Latium and Campania. Etruscan power was impressive, but the city-states, although mutually aligning themselves for economic and political gain, never united to fully coordinate their policies. The threatening power of Etruria eventually drove Romans, whose city was allegedly once ruled by the Etruscan Tarquin dynasty, and Greeks together against it. Trade rivalry resulted in a Greek-Etruscan battle of Alalia (535 BC), leaving Corsica in the Etruscan sphere of influence, but in 474 BC an allied Etruscan fleet was defeated off Cumae by a Syracusan fleet. A later effort to control the seaways saw the Etruscan League allying with Athens against Syracuse in a disastrous assault in 413 BC. The gradual weakening of Etruria saw a series of piecemeal conflicts between individual Etruscan cities and the growing power of Rome initiated by the fall of Veii (396 BC) after a ten-year siege. By 283 BC Rome had conquered Etruria, and by the reign of Caesar Augustus the region was becoming increasingly romanized.

Etrurian wealth was originally based on iron, which attracted Phoenician and Greek traders. The Etruscan city of Spina on the Adriatic traded with Istria and the Greek Dalmatian colonies. Contacts were made with La Tène Celts in Gaul and the mercantile network included trade with Tartessos, and Ampurias near Barcelona in Spain. This thriving commercial and agricultural civilization was mirrored by artistic and architectural achievements, eventually incorporated into the Roman tradition. House-styles were later copied in Rome, with colonnades around a courtyard with gabled or flat roofs decorated with terracotta statuary, as at the Etruscan site of Pogo Civitate near Siena. Their design has been found on ceramic votive models. Etruscan tombs repeat the design of houses, some being built above-ground and covered with earth tumuli, while others were dug into volcanic rock. The excavation of these tombs revealed many valuable artifacts, which allow archaeologists to reconstruct Etruscan life. Pottery developed a distinctive black bucchero ware with incised designs or with decorations in relief. Bronze work was particularly fine, including temple tripods, bowls and candelabra for divination in religious ceremonies. The Etruscans also made gold, silver and ivory jewellery, particularly gold earrings and wreaths of gold ivy leaves. Despite being defeated by Rome, many Etruscan practices continued in the forms of frescoes and reliefs, architecture and a peculiar sombrero-style hat that is still worn in the Sienese countryside.

ETRUSCAN EXPANSION

- Etruscan territory, before 600 BC
- Etruscan territory, early 6th century BC
- Etruscan territory, c. 600–474 BC
- Etruscan territory, c. 550–400 BC
- limit of Etruscan control, c. 530 BC
- Greek city-states, mid-6th century BC
- limit of Roman control, 380 BC

THE HALLSTATT CULTURE – THE CELTS I

The Hallstatt Celtic culture (750–450 BC), named after a burial ground in the Salzkammergut in Austria, spread its Iron Age technology and civilization throughout the Balkans, central Europe, France and Spain. Archaeological evidence suggests that these Celts probably began to settle in Britain. Artifacts recovered at the Hallstatt necropolis demonstrate elaborate funeral rites, whether by cremation or interment. Some graves contain four-wheeled carts and bronze harness mounts and bits, suggesting economic and cultural links with the Russian steppes, whether by origin or by the absorption of peoples moving westward from a steppe homeland. Finely decorated burial sites in Bohemia, complete with Greek wine amphora and pottery, in southern Germany and in northeastern France would appear to be those of chieftains.

The increasing utilization of iron and technological skills in its work mark the Hallstatt Age. However, this culture continued to use Bronze Age materials and techniques of the earlier Urnfield culture. The widespread use of iron allowed the Celts to fell forests and clear land for agriculture as well as engaging in raids and warfare among themselves or with other peoples such as the Iberians, who settled in the Iberian Peninsula. An indication of increasing warfare can be found in the construction of strongly fortified settlements and the later hill forts. The first fortified "castle" of the late Hallstatt period was found at Heuneburg on the Danube, where rich grave finds were uncovered.

This design of horse and rider is part of an elaborately decorated sword scabbard excavated at the Salzkammergut graves, Hallstatt. It shows a well-equipped cavalryman, armed with a lance, off to do battle.

The wealth of Celtic chieftains is well demonstrated by the interred works of art. Greek bronze, northern amber, gold and wine vessels point to an increase in trade. Greeks certainly acted as merchants at Massilia (Marseille). The grave furniture of an aristocratic young woman at Vix, near Châtillon-sur-Seine in the Côte d'Or, contained a five-foot-high bronze wine container (krater), emphasizing the importance of trade between the Hallstatt Celts and Greece. Other sites provide evidence of links with the Etruscan civilization in Italy. During and after the heyday of Hallstatt culture, there is evidence for an increase in salt extraction, both for domestic use and as a trade product, as is demonstrated by the Hallstatt mines with shafts that reach a depth of 1,300 feet.

Despite a prevalence of intertribal rivalry, the Hallstatt Celts made a great contribution to European art, inheriting their techniques from the Urnfield culture and thus laying the foundations for the flowering of art during the La Tène Celtic period. Hallstatt artifacts were generally decorated with repeated, rigidly designed, symmetrical geometric patterns, as can be seen on the pottery vessel in the Württermbergisches Landesmuseum in Stuttgart. Their stylization of chevrons and curves derives from the Scythians and other steppe peoples, but this did not preclude the Hallstatt Celts from occasionally creating artwork with images of animals and people. A thirty-five-cm-long vehicle was found at Strettweg in Austria, this comprising a group of bronze figures on a wheeled platform. In the centre stand a goddess surrounded by mounted warriors and sacred animals, including a horned god.

As far as Hallstatt Celtic society is concerned, it seems that it was made up of tribes and subdivided into families, with loyalty being accorded to the chieftain. Society comprised chiefs, warriors, druids, craftsmen, farmers, servants and slaves. The burial at Vix appears to show that aristocratic women were given parity with men, this being sustained by the existence of Boudicca, queen of the Iceni in a later period in Britain.

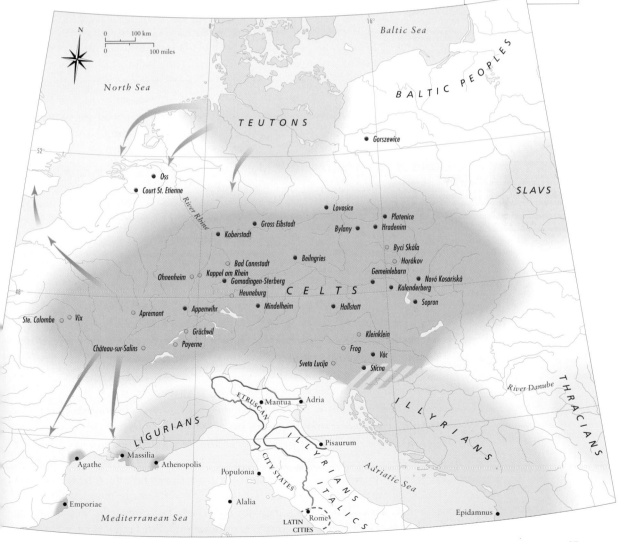

THE HALLSTATT CULTURE

SLAVS   people

→   Teutonic expansion

→   Celtic expansion

●   early Hallstatt site

○   late Hallstatt site

PART II: THE MEDITERRANEAN WORLD

Far right: This terracotta tablet shows a woman preparing a trousseau for a forthcoming marriage ceremony, and dates from the 5th century BC.

The rise of the city-state *(polis)* in the eighth century BC became a key feature in the spread of Greek civilization. It has been said that the city-state, a small, politically independent community of citizens who were protected by a fortified citadel, was a natural product of Greek physical geography, for the Greek Peninsula was a mountainous land with small coastal plains and valleys separated by mountains. Between the eighth and the seventh centuries, the economy, technology and culture flourished, with notable contributions in the field of Greek epic literature and lyrical poetry, provided by Homer and Hesiod.

The feeling that the city-states were united by a common Greek identity, based upon culture, language and religion, was best demonstrated by the foundation of the Olympic Games, in 776 BC, yet despite this the city-states engaged themselves in a state of almost perpetual conflict, most notably between Athens, Sparta, Thebes and Corinth.

During the same period, economic and social developments, boosted by colonial expansion took place, enhancing the importance of the Greek nobility. Yet by about 600 BC a transfer of power from the nobility to the citizens took place, which was particularly demonstrated in the military sphere of society, with the creation of heavily armoured infantry units, the Hoplites, among the wealthier citizens.

Although the Greeks had been hemmed in from the north by the Celts, colonial expansion gradually took place in Eretria, Chalcis, Corinth and Megara in central Greece; in Miletus in Asia Minor and the island of Rhodes, it was stimulated by Greek military superiority, land hunger and a desire for increasing trade and profit. Around the shores of the Mediterranean, Greek settlements were also established in Marseille (Massilia), Naples (Neapolis), Byzantium and Syracuse, which would become lasting centres of trade. The Greeks would learn much from their contacts with other cultures around the eastern shores of the Mediterranean, which would in turn influence their technical and philosophical development.

The Greek religion was centred upon the twelve Olympian gods, whose home, according to Greek mythology, was on Mount Olympus, the highest mountain in Greece. Here Zeus, "the father of all gods and men", held sway over the other deities and mortals in what can be described as a patriarchal system of hierarchy. The main deities were introduced by the Dorians who had invaded from the north. Each of the gods governed a variety of activities and human experience, as well as lying at the heart of Greek mythology, about whom a raft of stories of relations between the gods and ordinary mortals were recounted, forming the basis of classical Greek literature. The Olympian gods would in turn influence Roman religious beliefs, thinking and practice.

Another aspect of the Greek religion was the oracle, of which the most important was the Delphic Oracle, presided over by the god Apollo, who gave oracular utterance through the intermediary of a young priestess, the Pythia, who conducted her duties in a state of ecstasy. These oracles were

then translated by priests in charge and conveyed to the suppliant. Oracles formed an important feature of Greek cultural, social and even political life, and were used for advice on a variety of matters. The Delphic Oracle was usually consulted on the planning and conduct of military campaigns, and had even discouraged resistance to Persia, no doubt reflecting the attitudes of several influential Greek political advisors who wished to see Greece absorbed into the powerful Persian empire in 480 BC. Similarly, the oracle had given support to the Spartan cause against Athens, and during the period of Greek colonial expansion, the advice of the Delphic Oracle was also sought on where to site the new cities.

A limited form of democracy developed in the fifth century BC, although women, foreigners and slaves were denied political rights, against a backdrop of continuing conflict between the militarized state of Sparta and the democratic state of Athens, where every male citizen had the right to speak and vote in the assembly.

By the beginning of the fifth century, a new danger began to threaten the Greek city-states, which were obliged to unite to confront incursions from the Persian empire in 490 and 480. In the heat of battle, well-trained Greek Hoplites proved to be more than a match for Persian cavalry, who at the time were considered to be the best soldiers in the world. In the battle of Marathon in 490 BC, the phalanx of Athenian Hoplites, fighting at close quarters in a rigid formation of serried ranks, put the Persian troops to flight. Later, in 480 BC, three hundred Spartan Hoplites, led by Leonidas, king of Sparta, were able to hold a Persian army for a period of three days, before being defeated in action. It should be noted that the Persians were a hundred times superior to the Spartans in terms of manpower strength and had been led by their king, Xerxes.

In the meantime Athens grew in power as the leader of a free alliance of Greek maritime states, yet despite the period of unity brought about by the threat of Persian conquest, unity among the city-states was short-lived and a bloody war, known as the Peloponnesian War, soon broke out between Sparta and Athens, lasting twenty-seven years, between 431 and 404 BC.

The fifth century witnessed a further flowering of Hellenic culture, which has made a deep impact upon European civilization. This classical "Golden Age" was represented by historians, such as Herodotus and Thucydides; dramatists, such as Aristophanes, Aeschylus, Euripides and Sophocles; and the great philosopher Socrates, who would be followed in the fourth century by Plato and Aristotle, who worked together, as teacher and pupil, for a period of twenty years. Although scientific questioning had begun in the sixth century BC, influenced by contact with other cultures bordering the Mediterranean world, the greatest period of the kind of speculative thinking, argument and counter-argument that lie at the heart of the classical European philosophical tradition took place in the period between 550 and 400 BC. This period witnessed a growth in the number of sophists and professional teachers, who were a product of the

"The sense of wonder is the mark of the the philosopher. Philosophy indeed has no other origin."
Socrates

wealthy and leisured class that could be found in developing societies such as Athens.

Yet despite their thoughts upon the nature of Greek identity, Greece remained politically divided. Then in the mid fourth century, unity would be imposed upon the city-states by the rising power of Macedonia under Philip and later its great and able leader, Alexander, who compelled the Greek city-states to form an alliance with him prior to his attack on the Persian empire.

The military conquests of Alexander the Great had a huge impact upon the Hellenistic world, spreading Greek civilization from the Mediterranean shores deep into the heart of Asia. In 334, his combined Macedonian and Greek army of 35,000 men crossed the Hellespont into Asia Minor, winning the battle of the River Granicus and conquering all before them in Anatolia. They continued their advance upon Syria, defeating the main Persian army under Darius in 333 BC. With the conquest of Egypt, Alexander had gained control of the whole of the eastern Mediterranean and strategic control of the sea. Alexander's army then pushed east and southeast into Babylon and the Rivers Tigris and Euphrates, defeating Darius once and for all at the battle of Guagamel in 331 BC. The Greco-Macedonian forces then turned upon Persia, penetrating into the Hindu Kush, Bukhara and Tashkent. At its greatest extent, Alexander's empire spread as far as present-day Afghanistan and Baluchistan and northward into Bactria and Sogadiana.

A Roman stone funerary stele, made around AD 70, showing a cavalry soldier, spear held high, riding to attack.

Although Alexander had achieved such noteworthy military victories, he had totally failed to organize his empire politically. He had made no provision for his succession, so that on his death, in 323 BC, Alexander's huge empire broke up and was divided among his generals, who would fight among themselves for a period of fifty years. The ensuing rivalry and internecine strife throughout the third century BC eventually led to the development of a federal system among the city-states, of which the Aetolian and Achean leagues were the most prominent.

By the second century BC, great advances had been made in the expansion of trade by the Greeks with eastern Africa, Arabia, India, central Asia and even China. In the meantime, to the north, Rome, having conquered the whole of the Italian Peninsula south of the River Rubicon, including Etruria, began to threaten the borders of Greece. When Philip V of Macedon allied with the Carthaginian leader Hannibal in 215 BC, the Romans struck south, intervening in the Greek Peninsula for the first time.

By the end of the third century, the Roman republic had become the dominant military and political power in the Mediterranean, so that by mid second century it had effectively consolidated itself as an empire, although true imperial status would not be achieved until after the battle of Actium in 31 BC, when Octavian defeated the armies of Antony and Cleopatra, and was granted the title of Augustus by both the Senate and the people of Rome.

GREEK AND PHOENICIAN COLONIZATION

The Phoenicians were a Semitic people inhabiting a group of city-kingdoms on the eastern Mediterranean coast, the most important being Tyre and Sidon. After 1100 BC, the Phoenicians became prominent traders and sailors. Their fleets sailed throughout the Mediterranean and even into the Atlantic, founding many colonies, notably Utica and Carthage in North Africa, and on the islands of Cyprus, Sardinia and Sicily. Other Phoenician centres included the Balearics, Sexi in southern Spain and Tortessus (Gades) on the Spanish Atlantic coast to exploit silver, copper and tin deposits. Phoenician exports included cedar and pine, linen, material dyed with Tyrian purple, Sidonian embroidery, wine, metalwork and glass. Imports and transit goods included papyrus, ivory, Anatolian wool and Arabian resins and Cypriot copper, while Tyre formed an entrepôt for goods delivered down the Amber Road and by caravan routes to Memphis, Nineveh and Babylon, and hence to the Indus. Phoenicia eventually succumbed to a variety of imperial powers: Assyria, the Chaldean empire of Nebuchadnezzar II, Persia and Macedonia. The most significant contribution to civilization was the Phoenician alphabet, the probable ancestor of the Greek and thus all western alphabets.

Greek colonization paralleled the Phoenician, predicated upon demographic increase, the expansion of maritime

A vase decorated by a Greek immigrant from Ionia working in Etruria during the late 6th century BC.

THE PHOENICIANS AND GREEKS COLONIZE THE MEDITERRANEAN, 9TH–6TH CENTURY BC

- Phoenicia, c. 750 BC
- Phoenician settlement, from the 9th century BC
- Greece, c. 750 BC
- Greek settlement, 8th–6th century BC
- principal Phoenician colonizing cities
- principal Greek colonizing cities
- Greek or Phoenician colony

trade and social conflict. Colonies were founded by a mother-city but owned political autonomy, while keeping contact through common customs and religious cults. Expansion to the east was prevented by the growth of Middle Eastern empires, so colonization was focused on the western Mediterranean. After earlier colonization of the Black Sea, centres were established in Egypt, Cyrene, Sicily, Campania, southern Anatolia and southern France. These colonies eventually controlled the Black Sea grain trade and the tin route through Etruria. This Greek trade and cultural imperialism changed the whole complexion of the Mediterranean world. The Greeks imbibed ideas from Egypt, Mesopotamia and India, and developed their own synthesis, resulting in an unequalled flowering of culture, especially in Athens. New political structures were tested, from democracies to tyrannies, the latter exemplified by Dionysus I of Syracuse; the Ionians adopted a money economy, probably following Lydian examples, aiding the growth of a merchant class. In addition, art developed — by devising new forms of pottery; through drama writing by Sophocles and Euripedes; via comedies by Aristophanes; through the histories of Herodotus and Thucydides; and by schools of philosophy, forerunners of Socrates, Plato and Aristotle.

PELOPONNESIAN WAR

In 478 BC, the Delian League, a voluntary alliance, was established to drive the Persians from Greek city-states and the coastal islands of Asia Minor. Under the Athenian general Kimon, the Greek fleets defeated the Persians at Eurymedon in Pamphylia. Athens gradually dominated the league, and its members soon became subjects rather than allies, paying tribute instead of supplying ships to the league. Athens' tributaries became discontented under Athenian rule and rebellions occurred such as those at Naxos and Thasos, whose fortifications were destroyed in reprisal.

Under Pericles, Athenian imperialism became harsher, and Athens entered a Golden Age as a major artistic, architectural and cultural centre. However, Sparta led an alliance of independent states and had a stronger army than Athens, which possessed a superior fleet. Competition and conflict broke out but was ended by a Thirty Years' treaty (445 BC). In 433 BC, Athens allied herself with Corcyra, a Corinthian colony. When Sparta and its allies accused Athens of breaking the treaty, Athens stood her ground. The Peloponnesian War began when, in 431 BC, a Spartan ally, Thebes, attacked Plataea, an Athenian ally. The war can be divided into two distinct periods broken by a brief truce. The initial stage of the war saw annual Spartan incursions into Attica, which persuaded Pericles to withdraw his soldiers into Athens rather than facing superior military might. Instead, his fleets waged a campaign against coasts and ships. Crowded Athens suffered the plague, killing large numbers of soldiers and civilians, temporarily weakening Athenian morale. Elsewhere, Spartan attacks in western Greece were halted and an attempt to aid an anti-Athenian revolt on Lesbos was thwarted; the capture of Plataea (427 BC) was the sole success. Athens then took the initiative, moving into western Greece and the Peloponnese and interfering in Sicily, where Sparta and Athens

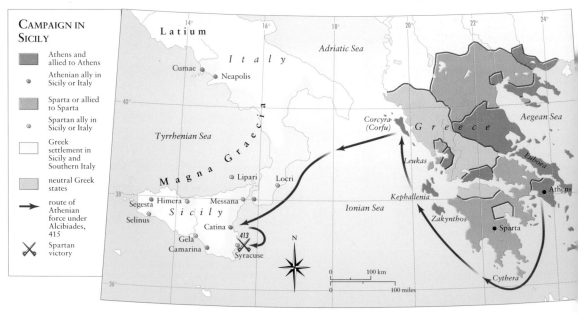

CAMPAIGN IN SICILY

- Athens and allied to Athens
- Athenian ally in Sicily or Italy
- Sparta or allied to Sparta
- Spartan ally in Sicily or Italy
- Greek settlement in Sicily and Southern Italy
- neutral Greek states
- route of Athenian force under Alcibiades, 415
- Spartan victory

supported different cities in an intra-island dispute. However, Sparta made important gains in Chalkidike, and defeated Athens at the battle of Amphipolis (422 BC). Exhausted, the enemies agreed on the Peace of Nikias (421 BC).

The war soon renewed, the Athenians suffering a major catastrophe in Sicily, where their entire force was destroyed (413 BC). A naval campaign was fought, with Athens gaining victories at Abydos (411 BC) and Cyzicus (410 BC), thereby securing the sea route to the Black Sea and its grain supplies. Events turned around when Athens suffered serious losses at Arginusae and the destruction of her fleet at Aegospotami (405 BC) by the Spartans. A further blow to Athenian prestige was the capture of Byzantium and Chalkedon, giving Sparta control of the Bosporus. A general revolt by Athenian allies broke out and Athens was rapidly placed under siege by both land and sea. Starvation forced Athens to capitulate, her Long Walls and those of Piraeus were destroyed and she submitted to rule by a Spartan-sponsored oligarchy known as the Thirty Tyrants (404 BC). Similar rule was established throughout the cities and islands of Asia Minor; Spartan rule was found more oppressive than Athenian. In 403 BC, an Athenian exile, Thrasybulus, liberated Athens, expelled the Spartan garrison and restored Athenian democracy and independence.

PELOPONNESIAN WAR, 431–404 BC

Athens and members of the Delian League, c. 431 BC

Athens's allies

→ Athenian campaign

✕ Athenian victory

Sparta and Spartan allies, c. 431 BC

→ Spartan campaign

✕ Spartan victory

✵ revolt against Athens

Persian empire

neutral states

THE RISE OF MACEDONIA

Macedonia (359–336 BC) achieved major historical importance during the reign of Philip II. On returning to Macedonia after being a hostage in Thebes, he reorganized his army into a mixture of cavalry regiments, a phalanx of infantry armed with pikes (*sarissa*), javelin throwers and archers. These were coordinated in battle in mutually supporting positions. Philip quickly reduced internal opposition (358 BC) after he usurped the throne and then sought to expand his kingdom's borders to secure improved access to the sea. In 357 BC, he captured the Athenian colony of Amphipolis in Thrace, acquiring the gold mines of Mount Pangaeus, which helped finance subsequent military adventures. Rapid military campaigns and conquests followed: Potidea in Chalcidice and Pydna on the Thermaic Gulf; Thracian Cremides; and Methone, with an advance into Thessaly. By 348 BC, Philip had conquered Thrace and Chalcidice.

A beautifully decorated golden quiver from the royal tomb of King Philip II of Macedonia, showing soldiers in action, made around 340 BC.

In 346 BC, Macedon and Athens (which had been defending its Chalcidian ally Olynthus against Philip) made the Peace of Philocrates. Philip then intervened in a war between Thebes and Phocis; his victory and replacement of Phocis in the Amphictyonic League gave Macedonia the right to participate in Greek political issues, while making Philip commander of the league forces.

The spread of Macedonian power spurred Demosthenes to attack it in his oratorical *Philippics*, warning of Macedonia's control of the grain route into the Black Sea. The subsequent alliance between Athens and Thebes was crushed by Philip at Chaeronea (338 BC) making him the master and arbiter of Greece. Philip organized the League Council of Corinth of all Greek cities, except Sparta and while preparing to invade Persia, he was murdered.

Philip undoubtedly laid the foundations for his son, Alexander the Great, to consolidate the control of Greece and then to construct a vast empire in the east. On his accession, Alexander immediately executed those accused of his father's murder, together with all possible rivals and opposing factions. His ruthless methods, unexpected in a former pupil of Aristotle, continued with an advance to the Danube to kill and burn out the Getae, the crushing of an Illyrian invasion and then a move south to put down a Theban and Athenian revolt. Thebes was razed to the ground; thousands were killed and the rest sold into slavery. Other dissenting states submitted and accepted Macedonian garrisons. In 334 BC, Alexander crossed the Hellespont into Asia Minor, defeated the Persian armies, captured Syria and Egypt, campaigned into Afghanistan and Uzbekistan and invaded the Punjab into the Mauryan empire. In 325 BC, his troops demanded a return, but Alexander died (323 BC) aged thirty-three years, leaving his commanders to carve up his empire into Macedonia, the kingdom of Antigonus in Asia Minor, Ptolemaic Egypt and the Seleucid empire.

Alexander was important in spreading Greek culture and language as far as India and establishing multi-ethnic cities based on equal rights for Persians and Greeks. New foci of culture and learning were established at Antioch,

Pergamon and Alexandria, and trade between the Mediterranean, the Near East and India was vitalized. Alternatively, Alexander might be seen as a megalomaniac, dying while dreaming of expanding into the western Mediterranean and the Carthaginian sphere of influence.

THE RISE OF MACEDONIA

- core area of Macedonian control, early 4th century BC
- added to Macedonia by 359 BC
- added to or subdued by Macedonia by 336 BC
- added to or subdued by Macedonia after 336 BC
- probable extent of the Corinthian League from 337 BC
- other Greek states

LA TÈNE CULTURE — THE CELTS II

Bronze brooch from Iberia showing a horseman carrying a severed head.

The La Tène culture, named after a Celtic archaeological site on Lake Neuchâtel in Switzerland, existed from about 450 BC to the conquest of Gaul by Julius Caesar in 58 BC. During this period many Celts left their homeland to cross the Alps and settle in the fertile river valleys of northern Italy, fighting and destroying many Etruscan cities on their way. In 38 BC, the Celts sacked Rome and raided down to Sicily; the Romans eventually recovered under Marcus Furius Camillus and drove the invaders back to the Alpine foothills. The Celts next enlarged their control in Europe, with incursions into central Europe, the Carpathians and the Balkans. The Roman historian Livy, as well as recounting the sack of Rome, describes how branches of the Celts settled in southern and central Germany. Under their leader, Brennus, they stormed into Bulgaria, Thrace and Macedonia. In 279 BC, Brennus fought the Greeks and looted the temple of the god Apollo at Delphi. Eventually, the Celts were driven out. After this defeat, surviving Celts built a fort on the eventual site of Belgrade, and one band crossed the Dardanelles into Anatolia, where they settled, giving their name to Galatia. Some even reached the Sea of Azov in Russia. Eventually, the Celts were squeezed between the military might of Rome and the pressure of expanding German tribes, which forced many Celts to the south and west, where later they would be conquered by the Romans; the absence of political unity contributed to the Celts' ultimate downfall. The La Tène culture in Britain was brought under Roman control in the first century AD. In time, the remnants of Celtic tradition and languages survived in Brittany, Cornwall, Wales, the Isle of Man, Ireland and the Highlands of Scotland — recently described as the Celtic fringe.

The La Tène culture developed the Hallstatt art forms and incorporated Greek and Etruscan styles but eventually Celticized these into its own legendary animals, plant motifs and human masks. The designs appeared on military accoutrements, bowls and vessels and mirrors. Examples of Celtic art are neck rings (torcs), broaches and particularly the silver Gundestrup cauldron (in the Danish National Museum in Copenhagen), on which the figures were hammered out from behind using the repoussé method. Other well-known finds are in the British Museum, including a bronze lozenge-shaped shield with medallions and enamel work and a bronze mirror with enamel decorations. In Britain and Ireland, La Tène art acquired a different style, especially in metalwork such as the Tara broach and Ardagh chalice.

The legacy of the Celts is considerable. They were christianized during the fourth century and were under immense pressure during the fifth-century invasions of Britain by pagan Angles and Saxons (after the Romans had left). This forced the Celtic

Christians into Ireland, Wales and Cornwall, with St. Patrick founding the centre of Christianity in Ireland. Irish monks preserved knowledge by keeping learning and the Christian religion alive. The manuscripts they created are beautifully illuminated, such as the *Book of Kells,* while the Celtic crosses surviving in Ireland and the Isle of Man have a beauty of their own, most notably the Manx examples at Maughold, on an ancient monastic site.

A second inheritance is the survival of Celtic literature and stories. Although the Celts did not write, they passed on law, history and stories through the oral tradition and parts of these are preserved in the Welsh *Mabinogion,* the Irish legends of Cuhulainn and the story of Bricriu's Feast.

ROOTS OF ROME, 753 BC

Since its foundation in 735 BC and for a period of nearly two and a half centuries, Rome would remain within the Etruscan sphere of influence, growing from a cluster of villages in the region known as Latium, into a city-state. This was the period before recorded history, bathed in myths about a Roman descendency from the fall of Troy; myths that were played to the accompaniment of the saga of Dido and Aeneas and the story of Romulus and Remus, who were suckled by a she-wolf, against the background of the rape of the Sabine women and the rape of Lucretia.

Dominated initially by the Etruscans in the north, with Greek settlements in the south of the Italian peninsula, Rome commanded a strategic crossing point of the River Tiber, the fullest-flowing river in central Italy. For a period of two centuries, the Romans extended their power over one tribe after another — Sabines, Aequi and Volsci — ultimately gaining ascendancy over the Etruscans.

The last Etruscan king, Tarquinius Superbus (the "Proud"), was overthrown in 510 BC, and Rome became a republic, governed by two consuls who were elected on an annual basis. Nevertheless, Rome's position remained insecure and Tarquin, with the help of the Etruscan leader, Lars Porsena, returned in a bid to retake Rome, only to be beaten off, according to Livy, by Horatius' heroic stand on the Tiber bridge. Rome would be joined by the other Latin cities, which by the major victory of Aricia in 506 BC, were eventually able to win their political independence from the Etruscans.

Now an important city, Rome was, during the fourth century, able to expand its power southward and throughout the Italian Peninsula, absorbed by warfare and diplomacy. Eventually the Romans defeated their one-time allies the Samnites, in the Second and Third Samnite Wars of 327–304 and 298–290 BC.

By 266 BC, the Romans controlled the whole of the Italian Peninsula south of the River Rubicon, spreading Roman citizenship throughout the region. By the middle of the third century BC Rome, having behaved as an expansionist power, united all of Italy, by defeating Pyrrhus, king of Epirus, in northwestern Greece, between 282 and 272 BC. The Romans consolidated their hold on the Italian Peninsula. In the second century BC, the Roman army crossed the straits of Messina onto Sicily and in so doing faced a new enemy, Carthage.

Bone tablets from Palestrina in Italy, carved during the 4th century BC, give a clear idea of the arms and personal equipment of Roman soldiers of the period.

ROOTS OF ROME

- Roman territory, 298 BC
- Samian League, 298 BC
- acquired by Rome to 263 BC
- Roman colonies, 272 BC
- Roman controlled by 270 BC
- Carthaginian possessions, c. 260 BC

A L P S

C E L T S

I L L Y R I A N S

LIGURIANS

Ligurian Sea

Pisae

Arretium
Volaterrae

Sentinum

Etruria

Aurinia

Volsinii

Asculum

Hadria

Cosa

Nepet

Falerii

Volci

Caere

Tibur

Alba Fucens

Rome

Praeneste

Ostia

Latium

Interamna

Arpino

Lucera

Tarracina

Suessa

Saticula

Camusium

Venusia

Cumae

Capua

Beneventum

Neapolis

Metapontum

Tarentum

Brundisium

Corsica

Aleria

Sardinia

Caralis

Tyrrhenian Sea

Thurii

Adriatic Sea

Ariminum

Ancona

River Rubicon

Rhegium

Locri

Strait of Messina

GREEK

y

CITIES

Syracuse

Panormus

Lilybaeum

S i c i l y

Utica

Carthage

Cossyra

0   50 km

0   50 miles

N

PUNIC WARS

Once the Romans had conquered the whole of the Italian Peninsula south of the Rubicon, they became involved in a series of three wars against the Carthaginians (*Poeni* in Latin). The first Punic War (264–241 BC) was largely waged at sea, which at first disadvantaged Rome, since Carthage was a maritime power, whose skilled sailors had extended its commercial interests in the western Mediterranean, establishing settlements in North Africa, Sicily and Sardinia. Although successful when fighting on land in Sicily, Rome would take a further eight years to secure victory over the Carthaginians in a sea battle off the Aegates Islands in 241 BC. By now, Rome had built a large fleet of warships and had mastered naval skills, enabling them to drive the Carthaginians first from Sicily, then from Corsica and Sardinia (238 BC).

During the second Punic War (218–201 BC), because the Romans had gained undisputed control of the Mediterranean sea routes, the famous Carthaginian general Hannibal marched across the Alps from the Carthaginian base in Spain. With a large army of 20,000 infantry and 6,000 cavalry, supported by sixty elephants and reinforced by Gallic tribesmen, he forced his way south into Italy, defeating a number of large Roman armies over a period of sixteen years' fighting, although he failed to capture Rome. When elephants were used against unprepared troops, they easily created panic; however, at the battle of Zama in 202 BC, the Roman commander Scipio, using experienced soldiers, was able to stand firm against Hannibal's elephants, which in turn bolted and ran amok among the Carthaginian forces, adding to their crushing defeat. Eventually, the Romans conquered Spain, which they divided administratively into two Roman provinces, and the Carthaginians were obliged to pay war indemnities and surrender their navy to Rome.

This detail from a 3rd century pottery dish from Campania shows an elephant, probably Indian, carrying soldiers and a "driver" equipped for war.

Fearful that Carthage was beginning to develop once more as a commercial power, the Senate and Roman public opinion, influenced by Senator Cato, once more went to war against Carthage. In the third Punic War, Carthage resisted a Roman siege for two years, but was eventually defeated and in 146 BC its territory was annexed as the province of Africa. Then, to ensure that its old rival would never again be a threat to Rome, the city was destroyed, its surrounding lands ploughed up, the furrows sown with salt and its population sold into slavery. Roman hegemony now spread along the Mediterranean to Sicily, Sardinia, Spain and Tunisia. Rome became involved in several wars with the Macedonians; Rome's status as a Mediterranean superpower was now confirmed.

PUNIC WARS

First War, 264–241 BC

- controlled by Rome, 264 BC
- controlled by Carthage, 264 BC

Second War, 218–201 BC

- added to Carthage by 218 BC
- conquered by Rome by 201 BC

→ Scipio's campaign, 218–210 BC
→ Roman campaign against Macedonia, 216–211 BC
→ Hannibal's campaign, 216–203 BC
→ Hasdrupal's campaign, 208–207 BC
→ Mago's campaign, 205–203 BC
✕ battle

Third War, 149–146 BC

- annexed by Rome by 121 BC

43

ROME — FROM REPUBLIC TO EMPIRE

During the last two centuries BC, Rome became the dominant military and political power in the Mediterranean, consolidating itself as an empire, although it was only at the end of that period that the title of emperor was adopted under Octavian. The rise of the Roman empire was brought about by military conquest and growing economic wealth and the concomitant rise of a series of powerful generals who jostled for power in an attempt to become single ruler, thus pushing the republic toward dictatorship during the last century BC.

These military dictators were: Sulla (138–78 BC), Pompey (106–48 BC) and Julius Caesar (100–44 BC). Sulla established himself as dictator of Rome with absolute power in 82 BC, when he defeated all political opposition. He later abdicated in 79 BC, and a struggle for succession took place between younger rivals, most famous of whom was Pompey, who engaged in a series of campaigns in Spain in the 70s BC. Pompey would reach the height of power in the following decade.

In the meantime, Julius Caesar was appointed governor of northern Italy and southern France in 59 BC; he invaded Gaul and led two reconnaissance operations to Britain in 55 and 54 BC. Caesar defeated Vercingetorix, leader of the Gallic confederacy, at the battle of Alesia in 52 BC. Caesar could now turn his attention to seizing supreme power in Rome itself.

Caesar crossed the Rubicon in 49 BC, leaving the boundary of Cisalpine Gaul to march south against the senatorial party and occupy Rome. Then he marched against Pompey, his chief rival, engaging his forces in combat, first at Dyrranchium, then at Pharsalus in Thrace, forcing Pompey to take flight into Egypt, where he was murdered. Caesar achieved supreme

Julius Caesar, the conqueror of Gaul and member of the Triumvirate. After many campaigns, he appointed himself perpetual dictator. He was assassinated after only a month on 15 March, 44 BC.

ALESIA, 52 BC

- Celtic fortifications
- Vercingetorix's positions
- Celtic attack
- Celtic retreat
- Roman wall
- Roman redoute
- Roman position

main attack of relief army

R. Rabutin

0 — 100 m
0 — 100 yds

cavalry

infantry

cavalry

R. Ose

Alesia

last sortie

cavalry

Celtic relief army

R. Brenne

cavalry

R. Oserain

Caesar's probable position during last battle

infantry

400
300
0 m

N

CELTS

Nemetocenna

Samarobriva

Noviodunum

Agedincum

Ale

Gau

conquest of Gaul by completed by 53

Gallia Ir

Brigantium

IBERIANS

R. Ebro

Burdigala

Vie

Tolosa

Gallia Ulterior

M

Hispania Ulterior

Salamantica

R. Tagus

Felicitas Julia

R. Guadiana

Toletum

Hispania Citerior

Tarraco

Dertosa

Palma

Balearic Islands

Hispalis

Corduba

Munda 45 BC

Carthago Nova

Tingis

Carteia

MAURETANIA

R. Moulouga

NUMIDIA

THE ROMAN EMPIRE, 55 BC

the first Triumvirate

- Caesar
- Pompey
- Crassus
- other Roman possessions
- allied to Rome

power as master of Rome after defeating the army of Pompey's sons at the battle of Munda (45 BC) but was himself assassinated the following year. Further civil wars broke out, eventually culminating in Octavian's seizure of supreme power over the whole Roman world by defeating the armies of Antony and Cleopatra at the battle of Actium in 31 BC. By this victory Octavian won acceptance from both the Senate and the Roman people at large, and in 27 BC, he was granted the title of Augustus with full support from the military, and the elimination of all political rivals in the Senate. He would be granted the status of god on his death.

ROME

aqueduct

wall

1 Templum Jovi Capitolini
2 Comitium with Curia Hostilia
3 Basilica Aemilia
4 Tabularium
5 Basilica Julia
6 Forum Julium

PART III: LEGACY OF ROME

The Roman empire had a lasting influence on European history. Rome was noted not only for its excellent army, which acted as the main guarantor of the empire, but also for its cultural and intellectual achievements. Its language, Latin, has provided the foundation of the Romance languages: Italian, French, Castillian, Catalán, Galego, Portuguese and Romanian. Latin served as the language of European diplomacy, until it was replaced by French in the early eighteenth century. It was also the main instrument of scholarly activity in parts of Europe until the nineteenth century and served as the language of the Christian religion well into the twentieth century. The literature of Rome, alongside the language, has been the mainstay of traditional European education well into the twentieth century.

The ruins of Roman settlements and works can be found from Britain to the deserts of Syria, from the Rhine to the upper Nile and Asia Minor. One of Rome's legacies, its laws, have inspired and influenced many European and non-European legal systems. Furthermore, despite the earlier persecution of Christians, Constantine the Great adopted the faith at the time of the battle of Milvian Bridge in 312; and under Theodosius, Christianity became the religion of state in 395. Christianity has remained, despite barbarian invasion, the dominant faith in most of Europe today.

The architects and planners in the cities achieved exceptional standards in street planning, buildings, central heating, aqueducts, dams, plumbing and sewage disposal. Rome's roads were crucial both to communications and to Rome's military needs across Europe and into Asia Minor and the Middle East. Long and straight, the lines of these roads have provided the foundation for many roads still in use today.

Rome had dominated the Mediterranean, both politically and militarily, during the last two centuries BC, and under Octavian (Augustus), Rome was transformed into an empire by the end of the first century BC. Augustus gave Rome strong centralized government, so that Rome could prosper, stimulated by wealth and trade and an economic and political shift westward from Greece, Egypt and Asia Minor. For the first two centuries AD, Italy flourished, as is demonstrated by the remains of great buildings, jewellery and other luxurious artifacts that archaeologists have unearthed from time to time.

Under Augustus, the northern Iberian Peninsula was conquered and the Danube became the frontier in the east. These conquests would continue throughout the first and second centuries, under Trajan (98–117) to Marcus Aurelius (168–180). Nevertheless, the second century became one of relative stability and consolidation; the period of great and gradual expansion came to an end.

The golden age of Rome came with the Antonines: Antonius Pius (138–161) and his adopted son Marcus Aurelius (168–180). During this period, Rome reached its greatest geographical limits. The Pax Romana now spread from the Atlantic to the Persian Gulf, with an almost stable frontier, with outbreaks of fighting in Asia against the Parthians and Persians, while the provinces were firmly controlled and protected within the *limes*, or frontier line, from Hadrian's

Wall to the Danube Delta.

Gradually, in the third century, Rome entered into a period of steady decline, with the exception of the reign of Diocletian (285–305), who introduced a series of reforms, restoring efficiency to government and laying the foundation of an empire in the east, which would last into the mid fifteenth century. By the late third and early fourth centuries, the eastern and western parts of the empire were growing apart and were confronted by different problems. Failure to defend the west against barbarian attack at the beginning of the fifth century was caused by the economic and social weaknesses of western Roman society. Large areas of the west were rural and underdeveloped and wealth lay in the hands of a few overmighty landowning families. By contrast, in the east, wealth was based upon trade in the cities around the Mediterranean, which had prospered in a climate where a more egalitarian society had developed; the gentry in the east, unlike their western counterparts, provided well-educated civil servants for the administration in Constantinople. Likewise, the rural peasantry was more independent than their western peers, who had more or less become serfs.

After the reign of Diocletian, the Roman army began to suffer from manpower shortages, which led to the employment of barbarian troops as *foederati*. Whereas the barbarian element in the eastern army was about 28 per cent, after the battle of Adrianople in 378, it was as high as 60 per cent in the western army. This led to a situation in which a Germanized army faced Germanic invaders in the west, whereas in the east, the army could draw upon Asia Minor for its manpower.

The Visigoths crossed the Danube frontier in 376 and advanced upon Italy. The Vandals marched into Gaul and Spain between 406 and 409. Rome was sacked in 410 by the Visigoths and later in 455 by the Vandals and in 493 by the Ostrogoths. In the meantime, the Burgundians settled along the middle Rhône Valley after 430. Nevertheless, rather than being organized military campaigns, the barbarian invasions should be seen as great waves of economic migration, from the underdeveloped north to the rich lands around the Mediterranean. The conquering tribes were often divided against each other and their leaders wanted to become Roman and were quite prepared to desert their fellow tribesmen in order to attain this. The barbarian invasions greatly changed lifestyles in the west. By the late fifth century, most of the western provinces were virtually lost to the empire.

In the sixth century, Justinian tried to reunite the eastern and western portions of the empire, inspired by the ideal of a Christian Roman empire with the Mediterranean Sea at its epicentre. Although he re-established Roman control over those Germanic peoples who had settled in Italy, France, Spain and North Africa, Justinian can nevertheless be described as the last true Roman emperor, and his reign (527–656) marks the end of the Late Roman period and the beginning of the Byzantine empire, which, built upon its Roman foundations, would last until 1453.

Many attempts were made to emulate the power of ancient Rome, but nearly all failed and none lasted as long. The iconography of military achievement, such as the triumphal arch, was easier to copy. Above is the original plan for the Arch of Triumph in Paris. Begun by Napoleon in 1806, it was not completed until 1836.

IMPERIAL ROME

A detail from Trajans column showing Roman troops engaged in constructing fortifications.

Caledonia

Hibernia

Britannia
Inferior

Eboracum

Deva

Britannia
Superior

Isoa Silur

Noviomagus

Vetera

Colonia Agrippina

Germania
Inferior

Bonna

R. Rhine

Belgica

Gallia Lugdunensis

R. Seine

R. Meuse

Augusta
Treverium

Germania
Superior

R. Loire

Vindobona

R. Vltava

R. Danube

Carnuntum

Brigetio

Aquincum

Poro

Lentia

Noricum

R. Drau

Vindonissa

Pannonia
Superior

Pannonia
Inferior

Dac

Si

ATLANTIC
OCEAN

Aquitania

Emona

Mediolanum

Mursa

R. Garonne

R. Rhône

R. Po

Sirmium

Gallia Narbonensis

Italia

Dalmatia

Moesi
Superior

Arelate

Burnum

R. Minho

Legio VII

R. Ebro

R. Douro

R. Tagus

Lusitania

Tarraconensis

R. Guadiana

Corsica

Rome

R. Tiber

Macc

Epirus

Baetica

R. Guadalquivir

Balearic Islands

Sardinia

Mauretania Tingitana

R. Moulouga

R. Chelif

Mauretania Caesariensis

Lambaesis

Numidia

Carthago

Sicilia

Africa Proconsularis

Mediterranean Sea

N

0   200 km

0   200 miles

Octavian's victory at the battle of Actium in 31 BC ended both the Civil Wars and the Roman republic. Octavian was crowned as the first emperor and renamed Augustus; his reign, from 27 BC to AD 14, was one of relative calm, stability and peace and Rome began to prosper once more.

Augustus provided Rome with strong, centralized government, made up from a cross-fertilization of elements taken from the republican period amalgamated with the concept of monarchical power. Although the Senate continued to function, Augustus, as *princeps,* or first citizen, held supreme power through his control of the government. As a result power was handed on, spanning a long line of emperors until the last quarter of the fifth century. Despite the fact that Roman emperors were absolute autocrats, and worshipped as gods, the legions' eagles continued to retain the legend SPQR (Senatus Populusque Romanus, the Senate and People of Rome).

Under Augustus, northern Spain was brought under Roman control and in the Alps and Balkans the frontier was extended northward to the River Danube. However, in spite of attempts to expand the German frontier to the River Elbe, the *limes* was pulled back to the Rhine, where it would remain

"As the Emperor Antonius, Rome is my city and my country; but as a man I am a citizen of the world."
Antonius, Meditations

IMPERIAL ROME

- senatorial provinces under Caesar
- imperial provinces under Caesar
- imperial provinces after Augustus
- colonies and municipalities before Caesar
- colonies and municipalities under Caesar
- colonies and municipalities under Augustus
- legionary base
- fort
- main base for Imperial Navy
- provincial capital
- main road

*A Roman funerary relief
of the 2nd century AD,
showing a tavern scene
and a delivery of more
wine, gives a good
impression of daily life
across the empire.*

until the empire began to crumble four centuries later.

Interspersed between the reigns of two of Rome's most unpopular and notorious emperors, Caligula (37–41) and Nero (54–56), came that of the Emperor Claudius (41–54). Claudius' great achievement was the invasion and occupation of Britain in 43. Southern Britain was almost completely subjugated when the last serious revolt, led by Boudicca, queen of the Iceni, was crushed in 60–61. By the end of the first century, most of the island would be under Roman control, although under Hadrian (117–138) the Romans eventually consolidated their position in Britain by withdrawing to the defensive frontier running across northern Britain, from Bowness to Wallsend, and known later as Hadrian's Wall. With this act and the establishment of the German frontier on the Rhine and Danube, the great period of expansion came to an end.

The first and second centuries would be marked by four great emperors: Trajan (98–117), Hadrian (117–138), Antonius Pius (138–161) and Marcus Aurelius (168–180). Trajan mastered Dacia, in present-day Romania, by defeating its powerful ruler, Decabalus, in two wars between 101 and 102 and in 105. In 114, he turned his attentions eastward against the Parthians, conquering Armenia and later occupying Mesopotamia by 116, although he would be forced to abandon southern Mesopotamia in 117.

The golden age of Rome, known as the Antonine period, came with Antonius Pius and his adopted son Marcus Aurelius.

During the reign of Antonius, wars were fought in the northern British Isles, resulting in the building of the Antonine Wall, to the north of Hadrian's Wall, between the Clyde and the Forth. Likewise wars were fought in Mauretania and on the Danube frontier, while the Parthians were deterred in the east.

The greatest geographical extent of the empire and the apex of Roman achievement were realized during the reign of Marcus Aurelius, after which decline set in. The Pax Romana spread from the Atlantic to the Persian Gulf, with fighting in Asia against the Parthians and Persians, while the provinces were firmly controlled and protected within *limes* (frontier lines) from Hadrian's Wall to the Danube Delta, which was far away from the centre of the empire. This meant garrison life for the Roman army, with static rather than mobile armies, engaged in defensive warfare carried out from large fortified camps, smaller forts, frontier posts and watchtowers.

"Would that the Roman people had but one neck!"
Gaius Julius Caesar Germanicus-Caligula

Providing the provinces with adequate protection was a major preoccupation of the empire. A large proportion of the army was based on or close to the frontiers, with strongly constructed defensive works, like this stretch of Hadrian's Wall in northern Britain. It was built between AD 122 and 126 and was maintained until around AD 383.

DIOCLETIAN — THE EMPIRE REORGANIZED

DIOCLETIAN, THE EMPIRE REORGANIZED

	dioceses of the Prefecture of Gallia		dioceses of the Prefecture of Illyricus, Italia and Africa		dioceses of the Prefecture of Orient		Western and Eastern Roman empires border, 395

XII	Britannia	VI	Macedonia	I	Egypt
XIII	Gallia	VII	Dacia	II	Orient
XIV	Seven Provinces	VIII	Pannonia	III	Pontica
XV	Hispania	IX	Italia Annonaria	IV	Asia
		X	Italia Suburbicaria	V	Thracia
		XI	Africa		

province border

diocese border

N

0		200 km
0		200 miles

Diocletian, emperor between 285 and 305, is most remembered for having restored efficient government to the Roman empire after the troubled third century, during which time it had been weakened by internal faction and continuous attacks from external enemies. He temporarily re-established the decaying empire in the west and laid the foundation of the Byzantine empire in the east. It was during his reign that the last persecution of the Christians took place.

When Emperor Numerian was found dead in camp, during a campaign against the Persians, Diocletian was acclaimed emperor by his soldiers in 284. However, Diocletian's power base lay only with his army in Asia Minor, so he had to achieve power, first by putting down a revolt in Pannonia and then by the decisive battle against Numerian's brother and co-emperor, Carinus, near Sirmium (Belgrade) on the confluence of the Rivers Morava and Danube. As a result, Diocletian became master of the Roman empire in 285, first as caesar (junior emperor) and then, a year later, as augustus (senior emperor).

Given the vastness of empire, with disturbances on all the frontiers, Diocletian decided to share his throne with his friend Maximian in 286, thus dividing the empire administratively; Maximian was installed in Milan and granted the west, while Diocletian took responsibility for the east and based himself in Nicomedia, where he could keep watch on the Persian frontier.

In 293, power was divided yet again with two other colleagues, Galerius and Constantius, who were appointed to the rank of caesar. This relationship, known as the Tetrarchy, was bonded by marriage and strengthened by the belief that like Jove and Hercules, Diocletian and Maximian no longer were mere *princepes* but emperors and gods *(domini et dei)*. The empire took on the aspects of a theocracy, with Diocletian and Maximian exercising autocratic power based upon "divine right" and surrounding themselves with all the pomp and circumstance that would later become the hallmark of Byzantine imperialism.

The empire was still troubled by threats from external enemies. Maximian had to fight Carausius, who had declared himself emperor of Britain and reigned for nearly ten years before Constantius I reconquered Britain in 296. At the same time, revolts and disturbances had to be put down in Mauretania, the Danubian regions and Egypt. No sooner had Diocletian reconquered Egypt in 296, than he had to turn his attention to Syria which had been invaded by Narses, king of Persia, in 297. Galerius eventually won Syria back for the empire, so that the River Tigris became the eastern border of the empire.

Diocletian's vast administrative, military, judicial, fiscal and monetary reforms led to firm government, and a centralized and absolute monarchy, that witnessed the growing specialization of administrative work and a concomitant increase in the number of bureaucrats.

Diocletian's first task was to restore civil order to the empire by taking the army out of politics in a bid to improve internal security, so that the governors of the provinces no longer held any military authority. This meant putting an end to the constant threat of insurrection by powerful provincial governors, who had undermined the empire throughout the previous half century.

The provinces were then reorganized into twelve larger administrative units called dioceses. The army was also reorganized and traditional discipline reintroduced along with a reduction of military service to twenty years and moves toward greater efficiency and increasing the number of troops. Diocletian also introduced agricultural and building programmes and combated the inflationary financial crisis by levying taxes on a proportional basis, by fixing wages, establishing maximum prices and by introducing monetary reform, which included a return to sound gold and silver coinage.

Sick through overwork, Diocletian abdicated in 305, being the only Roman emperor to do so voluntarily. He retired to his birthplace in Split, present-day Croatia, where he constructed a stone-built palace and spent his last days until dying almost unnoticed, in 316.

While Angles, Saxons, and Jutes crossed the North Sea and invaded Britain from 450, other Germanic peoples migrated from southern Scandinavia into Germany, pressured by an increasing population and deteriorating climatic conditions.

By 300, the Goths reached the lower Danube and the Franks the middle and lower Rhine. About 370, the Goths divided into the Ostrogoths, in a kingdom east of the Dniester on the shores of the Black Sea, and the Visigoths, who inhabited an area from the Dniester to the Danube. Another group, the Vandals, settled along the Danube. Mounting demographic pressure occasioned wars with the Romans, and in 375, a momentous event occurred: Huns from central Asia attacked the Ostrogoths, causing immense fear and dislocation among the German tribes. In 376, the Visigoths sought the protection of Rome and were allowed to settle in imperial Moesia, where they were converted to Arian Christianity.

In the west, Germanic war bands continued to migrate into the empire. The empire, as in the past, absorbed them, granting them "federate" status; in return they agreed to perform a role in imperial defence, mostly aimed at preventing further of their relatives from entering, settling or raiding the empire. In reality however they ruled over the areas and people they were supposed to defend, forming kingdoms, power centres in their own right. Rome's taxation income fell and its ability to control its new allies and its own destiny declined.

This mosaic shows Bishop Ambrosius of Milan. High-ranking Christian clerics like him had immense power. In 390 Ambrosius even succeeded in making Emperor Theodosius do public penance.

GERMANIC KINGDOMS

In 395, the Visigoths renounced their allegiance to Rome, invaded Greece and then migrated to Italy. Meanwhile, the Vandals entered France (406) and invaded Spain (409). After the Visigoths sacked Rome (410), they crossed the Pyrenees into Spain where they fought the Vandals. Under their leader, Gaiseric, the Vandals moved to North Africa (429), defeated the Romans and captured Carthage (439), making it the capital of a Vandal kingdom. Gaiseric's fleets raided Sicily, Sardinia and Corsica, and in 455 entered Rome and looted it for two weeks before moving east to ravage Greece and Dalmatia, forcing Emperor Zeno to recognize Gaiseric and make peace (476).

In Spain, the Visigothic kingdom embraced most of the Iberian Peninsula and part of Provence with its capital at Toulouse. King Theodoric I died fighting Attila at Châlons (451) in alliance with Rome. King Euric declared the independence of Rome but introduced aspects of Roman civilization and codified a collection of German and Roman law. Visigothic kingship's elective nature ensured internal instability and although reducing a Suevi kingdom in north Portugal (469), the Visigoths were threatened by the Franks, whose king, Clovis I, defeated them at Vouillé (507) and took most of Provence, confining the Visigoths to Spain. When the Huns attacked Europe, they conquered many Ostrogoths, compelling them to join Attila in his French raid. The defeat at Châlons freed the Ostrogoths and they settled in western Hungary, northern Croatia, Serbia, Slovenia and eastern Austria, where they were joined by the king who had fled the Roman empire during the Hun invasion. Under Theoderic, the Ostrogoths invaded Italy (488), killed Odoacer, the first barbarian ruler of Italy and supplanted him. Theoderic used the Roman civil administration and economy, and Roman culture influenced the Germans, but the latter's Arian Christianity caused conflict with the Catholic Romans. Eventually Visigothic power was destroyed by the Byzantine empire (555). Other Germans settled near Lake Geneva, extending down the Rhône Valley. This Burgundian kingdom lasted from 443 to 534, finally being subjugated by the Franks. These Franks, who became Roman allies, established a kingdom north of the Loire. When Rome retreated, the Franks under Merovingian Clovis I became the most successful Germans, defeating the Alemanni, the Burgundians and the Visigoths in Provence. In 496, Clovis was converted to Christianity, commencing a special link between the Frankish monarchy and the papacy.

An engraved bronze plaque of a horseman, often used as a symbol by wandering Germanic tribes. Lombard, 7th century, from Stabio in Switzerland.

GERMANIC KINGDOMS,
c. 500

movements of peoples

→ Huns

→ Slavs

→ Germanics

→ Celtics

Norwegian Sea

FINNO-UGRIANS

Arctic Circle

Faeroe Islands

North Sea

C E L T S

Baltic Sea

SCANDINAVIANS

JUTES

ANGLO-SAXONS

ANGLES

SAXONS

FRISIANS

SLAVS

FRANKS

BURGUNDIANS

KINGDOM OF THE THURINGIANS

ALEMANNI

VANDALS

FRANKISH KINGDOM

HUNS

Lutetia

ATLANTIC OCEAN

Namnetes

KINGDOM OF THE OSTROGOTHS

KINGDOM OF BURGUNDY

SUEVES

VISIGOTHS

KINGDOM OF THE SUEVES

BASQUES

Pavia

Ravenna

Marcianopolis

Naissus

Black Sea

Arelate

Spalatum

EAST ROMAN EMPIRE

Massilia

Adrianople

Adriatic Sea

Constantinople

Toletum

KINGDOM OF THE VISIGOTHS

Corsica

Rome

Salonica

Lisbon

Sardinia

Aegean Sea

Valentia

Balearic Is.

KINGDOM OF THE VANDALS

Smyrna

Hispalis

Mediterranean

Panormus

Athens

Carthago Nova

Sicily

Hippo Regius

Carthage

Sea

Crete

VANDALS

B E R B E R S

59

THE EMPIRE IN THE EAST

This detail of a mosaic shows Justinian I, 483–565, who was Byzantine emperor from 527. He recovered North Africa from the Vandals, southeast Spain from the Visigoths and Italy from the Ostrogoths, largely owing to the skills of General Belisarius.

In 324, Emperor Constantine chose the old Greek settlement of Byzantium, which lay on the Bosphorus, as the site for a new city that would become the capital of the Roman empire in the east. As Constantinople — the city of Constantine — it served as a crossroads between Europe and Asia, opening up trade links between the Aegean, the Mediterranean and Asia Minor, to the Middle and Far East. Although the eastern part of the empire, or *pars orientalis*, was more densely populated and had greater economic resources than the west, the two parts of the empire held together in the fourth century, due to the reforms of Diocletian. The empire remained one and indivisible.

The two main external pressures came from a rival empire in Persia and from the Germanic tribes from the north. As with Diocletian, it was probably because the main threats to the empire came from the Danube and the eastern frontiers that Constantine chose to take control of the eastern half of the empire, leaving his co-emperor to rule in the west. The problems in the east gravitated around the conflict between eastern Rome and the Sasanian empire over the control of Syria, Palestine and Egypt.

Justinian is noted for the administrative reforms of the imperial government, for a concern for rooting out administrative corruption, and for the codification of laws, which are known as the Codex Justinianus, which formed the basis upon which later Byzantine codes would be built.

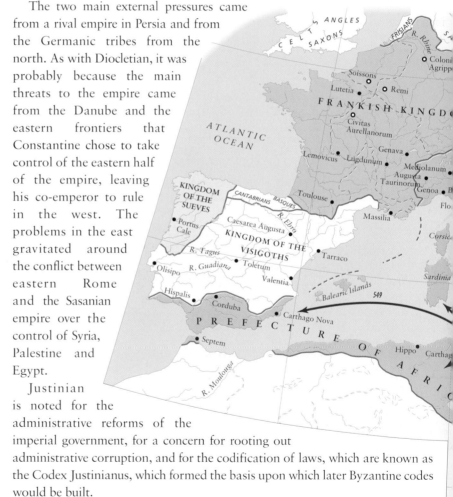

Justinian was inspired by the ideal of a Christian Roman empire that would be restored to its old boundaries and dominate the Mediterranean world, by re-establishing Roman control over the Germanic peoples who had settled in Italy, France, Spain and North Africa. The Vandals in North Africa were defeated by Justinian's general, Belisarius, in 533. Belisarius proceeded to fight against the Ostrogoths in the Italian Peninsula and the islands of the western Mediterranean.

These were finally conquered by Narses in 555. Meanwhile, a bridgehead was established in southeastern Spain, although most of the Iberian Peninsula, southern France and Gaul would remain in the hands of the Visigoths and other Germanic tribes.

In the east the Persian-Sasanid king Chosroes I invaded Mesopotamia, northern Syria and Byzantine Armenia in 540. Belisarius led counter-offensives in 541 and 542. The expensive military campaigning dragged on until 562, when a fifty-year truce was negotiated. On the northern frontier the imperial territories of Thrace, Dacia and Dalmatia were confronted by attacks from Bulgar, Slav and Avar invaders. Despite the building of forts and defence works, the invaders were neither assimilated nor were they repulsed. The problems of the Balkans would be left to Justinian's successors.

"We have good hope that God will allow us to reconquer the lands of the old Roman empire which have been lost through indolence."
Justinian

THE EMPIRE IN THE EAST

- the empire at the accession of Justinian, 527
- reconquered by Justinian to 565
- disputed territories
- Justinian's campaigns
- patriarchate
- metropolitan see
- major city or town

PART IV: CHRISTIAN EUROPE

The European mental condition prior to the fall of the Byzantine empire in 1453 was pervaded by a hankering after the perceived glories of Roman empire and the overwhelming spirit and influence of religion and faith.

Religion dominated every activity of life, both personal and political. The popularity of pilgrimages may be placed alongside the missionary activities throughout Europe, with the mass conversions of peoples and the spreading of the Gospel by "fire and sword". Ascetic hermits in isolation contrasted with the

This 15th century French illustration shows the Turkish fleet and army laying siege to Constantinople in 1453.

rise of collective monastic orders in the tenth century. Along with a belief in miracles and millenarianism came the superstitious fear of purgatory and the eternal fires of hell and damnation. Organized and centralized religion brought a sense of unity to western Christendom, powered by the universal usage of the Latin in both worship and legal procedure. Linked with the religious mood of the times was the growing cleavage between western Christendom and the Byzantine empire. Latin Christianity and Orthodoxy grew further apart and completely broke with the Schism of 1054, so that east and west would both go their own ways.

The Carolingian empire reinforced the power of both church and state, with obligatory tithes, the banning of pagan ceremonies, the death penalty for the murder of priests and a move toward centralizing political power. The link between the pope and the western emperor was established with the coronation of Charlemagne in 800. This action meant that there would be a Catholic emperor in the west, independent of Byzantium, emphasizing once again the increasing separation between east and west. The existence of two empires sounded the death knell of the ideal of a universal empire. From this time on, the pope would always crown the emperor. In the eleventh and twelfth centuries there arose the whole issue of the Investiture Controversy, which might have been the single most important issue of the central Middle Ages, for both the contemporary and long-term effect it had upon Europe, especially with regard to the Italian and German lands.

The Europe of the Middle Ages was also defined by external events and threats, especially those of the Vikings, the Magyars, the Mongols and the Turks. The Vikings would exploit the internecine strife of Charlemagne's successors, raiding the coasts and rivers of Europe; eventually this threat receded due to a combination of military preparedness and the Vikings themselves becoming settlers. The Magyars, beaten at the battle of Lechfeld in 955, were forced to retreat to the Pannonian Plain, which helped establish Otto I of Saxony's claim to supremacy as emperor over the German princes.

In the meantime, medieval European polity was based upon feudalism, the relationship or contract between a superior to a vassal, arising from the holding of lands in *feud* or in *fief*, a system by which land was held and protection offered in return for services, such as homage, obedience, duty and military service. There developed a whole hierarchical system of contracts, with individuals being tied to their masters and in turn having their own vassals, each with their own privileges and rights. Even the pope and the emperor were the vassals of God, with the serfs at the bottom of the ladder, labouring on the lord's *demesne* for so many days a year, fixed by local custom.

Later, during the twelfth-century renaissance, feudal society would be supported by the concept of "chivalry" — a code of knightly honour and gallantry based upon the understanding and practice of "courtesy", loyalty and bravery. This meant a respect for women and support for those weaker than oneself, along with obedience to one's lord, the protection of the church and the obligation to go to war against the infidel.

Throughout Europe the process of institutionalized Christianity continued. The first monastic order, centred on reforms of Benedictine rule, was founded at Cluny in Burgundy in 910. A network of over three hundred monasteries was created by the middle of the twelfth century. The more austere Carthusian Order, based upon silence, contemplation and closed cells, was founded in 1084 by St. Bruno at Chartreuse, and in 1098 the Cistercian Order was established at Citeux in Burgundy.

It can be said that the Saxon kings Henry II "The Fowler" (918–936), founder of the Saxon dynasty, and his son, Otto I "The Great" (936–973), were the successors of the Carolingian empire. Under Otto, the crown developed stronger links with the church, which became a pillar of the monarchy. The monasteries would act as centres of imperial power throughout the German duchies. By conquering the Italian lands and acquiring the imperial title, Otto recovered Germany from the anarchy of the late Carolingian period. His control of the papacy, whereby all popes had to swear allegiance to the emperor, and his dreams of re-establishing government in Rome, through his grandson Otto II (980–1002), meant that the German empire was the true successor to that of Charlemagne and would maintain a prominent position in Europe until the death of Frederick II in 1251, despite the impact of the Investitures Struggle between the empire and the papacy.

Otto had restored the empire, which would last until 1804, when the Holy Roman empire became the Austrian empire, when some of its territories fell under the threat of Napoleon's expanding French empire.

In the meantime, the Byzantine empire reached its political and cultural apogee in the late ninth and tenth centuries, under the emperors of the Macedonian dynasty. Constantinople's economic strength and its trade with the east continued to flourish, despite the growth in importance of some Italian maritime cities. Furthermore, Byzantium's links with Kievan Rus along the "Water Road" were increasing. The Byzantine empire also benefited from the existence of a highly developed civil service and an efficient system of provincial government. It even looked as though the Byzantines might themselves recapture the

Holy Places. Certainly at the beginning of the tenth century nobody would have entertained the idea that Byzantium would one day have to rely upon Latin crusaders to achieve this.

The situation in the Balkans was slightly different in that the Slavs were assimilated into the Balkans, although in the short term this meant the cities were isolated from the surrounding Balkan countryside. Gradually the Slavs fell under the military and political control of Byzantium and began to reach out for the fruits of Byzantine culture they so much admired. Ever since the development of an alliance between the papacy and the Frankish rulers in the eighth century, the Church of Rome and that of Constantinople had tried to win the Slavs for their particular part of the Christian Church. Serbia, Bulgaria and Russia would come under the influence of the patriarchate of Constantinople, while Croatia would fall under the influence of western Christendom, through the intermediary of Hungary.

The Orthodox faith spread throughout southeastern Europe, particularly through the missionary activities of Saints Cyril (827–869) and Methodius (825–884), whose main achievements in the history of the Balkans were the invention of Slavonic scripts, Glagolitic and Cyrillic and the spread of the Old Church Slavonic language, which became the main intermediary for transmitting Byzantine civilization to Bulgarians, Serbs, Romanians and Russians. The main task of Basil II was to dominate the northern part of the Balkan Peninsula. During his reign the Byzantine empire was prosperous and expanding and it could not afford to tolerate the power of the Bulgarian state on its frontier. Basil aimed for the control of the Macedonian mountains to consolidate the northern part of the peninsula. He downgraded the patriarchate of Ohrid and blinded 14,000 Bulgarians at the Kleidion pass in 1014. According to Obolensky, he left one in every hundred with one eye so that he could guide his comrades back to the Bulgarian tsar. From the second half of the eleventh century western Europe entered a period of "reform and revitalization", while the Byzantine empire began a period of "irreversible decline".

Setbacks in Byzantine fortunes would come toward the end of the eleventh century, with the Norman occupation of Sicily in 1071; the threat of the Seljuk Turks in Asia Minor, who that same year had routed a Byzantine army at the battle of Manzikert; the Pechenegs laying Constantinople to siege; and the arrival of the First Crusade in 1095.

Pecheneg pressure on Byzantium had been stimulated by events in Russia, when in 1036 Yaroslav had inflicted a defeat upon them, putting an end to their dominion over the steppes and forcing them to aim toward the Byzantine empire. Byzantium's links with Kievan Rus had been growing throughout the ninth century, through trade along the Water Road and the supply of military services to the emperor in Constantinople. In the tenth century, with paganism on the decline everywhere, Kievan Rus was becoming isolated. Eventually, Christianity was adopted in 988 by Vladimir (980–1015). The conversion had been politically inspired as a pragmatic necessity to end Russia's isolation and also to stimulate trade, thus introducing stronger Byzantine influences to Russia.

Nevertheless the process whereby the country experienced long and bitter quarrelling and infighting among the princes, on the death of each Grand Prince, exhausted Russia's resources. Trade was disrupted and people fled certain areas or invited foreign intruders for their protection. In many ways this contributed to the downfall of the Kievan state and the situation was exploited by the Tatars in the second half of the thirteenth century.

Meanwhile, in the eleventh century, the West witnessed the rise of wealthy, well-defined cities and urban societies, with their artisans' guilds and merchant associations. Alongside the formation of a new class, the burghers, was the rise of trade. Trade across the North Sea was based upon English wool, with key trading centres established in Bruges and Ghent. In the Mediterranean the control of trade gradually passed from Constantinople to Genoa and Venice, the latter becoming the key trading centre between east and west, while in Germany Lübeck and Hamburg became important trading centres on the Baltic.

The Crusade was first launched by Pope Urban II at the synod of Clermont in 1095, with an appeal to all Christians to win back Jerusalem from the Turks. There would be a variety of Crusades, one of the most curious, the Albigensian Crusade in twelfth-century Provence, was launched by Innocent III on the grounds of heresy and in response to their censure of the corruptions of the papacy. The Albigensians were dualist gnostics, who believed that only spiritual things belonged to God and that all things physical were of the Devil. If the western Church had its Albigensians, so the Orthodox Church attempted to wipe out the Bogomils and Patarenes in the Balkans, especially in Bosnia and Bulgaria.

Conflict between Christians and Muslims was not just confined to the Byzantine eastern frontier, nor was it just a concern of the Latin Crusaders, for it also affected Spain, much of which had fallen to the Moors in the eighth century. The Christian Reconquista of Spain began in 1085, when the Muslim city of Toledo fell to Alfonso VI of Castle-Léon, followed by the capture of Valencia by El Cid. So began four centuries of conflict between Christian and Muslim for control of the Iberian Peninsula. Already by the end of the thirteenth century, with the seizure of Córdoba (1236), Seville (1248) and Murcia (1266), the bulk of the Iberian Peninsula was in Christian hands.

Growing prosperity in Europe led to a desire for knowledge that resulted in an increase in scholarship and book production. Along with a growth in libraries came the spread of monasteries and the rise of the universities as centres of secular learning, the first at Bologna in 1088, then Paris c. 1150 and Oxford in 1167. Scholars gathered to hear the teachings of William of Malmesbury, Geoffrey of Monmouth, Adelard of Bath and others, while medical schools and law facilities were established at Salerno, Montpellier and Bologna. The classical texts of many scientific and philosophical writers had been preserved by the Arabs; these were retranslated into Latin and spread throughout western Christendom.

THE EMPIRE OF CHARLEMAGNE

Charlemagne, son of Pepin, who usurped the last Merovingian king, became sole king of the Franks in 771. His long reign was spent at war, amassing lands in what became a "Christian empire". As early as 772, he commenced the Saxon wars, which lasted until 804. During this conquest, the Saxons' sacred wood, the Irminsul, was destroyed and their nobility baptised en masse. The Christianization of the Saxons developed through the activities of bishoprics at Verden, Bremen, Paderborn and Hamburg. A Saxon March was established to keep the Danes in check. Meanwhile, Charlemagne invaded the kingdom of Lombardy, annexed it and assumed its crown (774), thereby placing the papal states under Frankish protection, since Lombardy had been devouring papal lands. The duchy of Spoleto south of Rome was also acquired in 774. In 778, the duchy of Bavaria was absorbed and Charlemagne continued the Bavarian policy of establishing tributary marches among the Slavic Serbs and Czechs. The remaining power confronting the Franks in the east were the Avars, but they were destroyed by a combined Franko-Bulgarian attack (796), and Charlemagne acquired further Slav areas, including Bohemia, Moravia, Austria and Croatia. His onslaught on the Umayyad Muslim caliphate in Spain achieved limited success, but a buffer Spanish March was established (795, and enlarged in 812) as a shield against a possible Muslim power revival. Charlemagne had built a mighty empire and in 800, Pope Leo III crowned him emperor, recognizing and formalizing political realities that all Christians inhabiting Europe, except the British Isles, owed allegiance to Charlemagne. His position was recognized by the Byzantine emperor Michael I by the 812 Treaty of Aix-la-Chapelle (Aachen) in exchange for Istria, Venice and Dalmatia.

This reliquary bust of Charlemagne, the man who became the first Holy Roman emperor, is from the cathedral treasury at Aachen.

Charlemagne placed his power and prestige in the service of Christianity. He encouraged monasteries and cathedrals to maintain schools and invited to his court scholars and writers from Ireland, England, Spain and Italy. Alcuin of York, later Abbot of St. Martin's of Tours, standardized writing, which aided improvements in teaching and helped revive Latin. These processes were useful in the copying of manuscripts of surviving classical works. The church benefited from a better-educated clergy and scholarship, and authors flourished; Einhard wrote his *Vita Karoli Magni*. Charlemagne utilized bishops and abbots as agents of government and established a more permanent royal capital at Aix-la-Chapelle, where his Palatine Chapel was consecrated. The emperor attempted to introduce vassalage as a system of government and the frontier marches comprised several counties as a means of controlling the tributary tribes inhabiting them. A major flaw in the empire was its personalized nature, and Charlemagne's decision to divide his territories among his three sons was frustrated by only one surviving him. Louis the Pious continued the scheme and the Frankish empire was finally fragmented into three parts by the Treaty of Verdun (843). The descendants of Carolingian royal agents tended to identify with their localities, stressing a movement toward feudalism. The empire was weakened by a minimalist administration and was seriously damaged by Viking raids, which had begun during Charlemagne's lifetime.

THE EMPIRE OF CHARLEMAGNE, 814

- Frankhish empire
- Frankish subject
- *SLAVS* tribe

ARAB CONQUEST OF IBERIA, 711–732

- → main Arab campaign, 711–732
- under Arab control by c. 732
- unconquered Iberian peoples, c. 732
- Frankish kingdom, c. 732

(Inset map: Arab Conquest of Iberia)

FRANKISH KINGDOM
BRITTANY
Sens
732 Poitiers
Lyons
ATLANTIC OCEAN
Bordeaux 732
CANTABRIANS
BASQUES
raids 713–25
Oporto
Zaragoza
Narbonne 719
Barcelona
VISIGOTHIC KINGDOM
Lisbon 716
Toledo 712
Valencia 714
raids from 714
Balearic Is.
Seville 712
Córdoba 711
Algeciras 711
ARAB CALIPHATE

(Main map)

Norwegian Sea
Arctic Circle
SCANDINAVIANS
Kaupang
Birka
North Sea
Baltic Sea
BALTIC PEOPLES
R. Vistula
SCOTTISH KINGDOMS
KINGDOM OF PICTS
STRATHCLYDE
NORTHUMBRIA
Lindisfarne
York
IRISH KINGDOM
WELSH STATES
MERCIA
London
WEST WALES
WESSEX
DENMARK
Ripen
Hamburg
Frisland
Saxony
Aachen
R. Rhine
Hessen
Frankfurt
Bohemia
SLAVS
France
Mainz
Nordgau
Moravia
R. Dniester
Paris
Metz
Strasbourg
Bavaria
Britanny
FRANKISH EMPIRE
Alamannia
Carinthia
Pannonia
R. Danube
AVAR EMPIRE destroyed 791
ATLANTIC OCEAN
Aquitaine
Geneva
Italian Kingdom
Milan
Dalmatia
BULGARIANS
Bordeaux
Lyon
Turin
Venice
Varna
Burgundy
Genoa
Ravenna
SLAVS
Nish
Toulouse
Septimania
Marseille
Adriatic Sea
Ragusa
Constantinople
ASTURIAS
Spanish March
Corsica
Papal States
Rome
PRINCIPALITY OF BENEVENTO
VLACHS
Salonica
Oporto
Barcelona
BYZANTINE EMPIRE
Aegean Sea
EMIRATE OF CORDOVA
Balearic Is.
Sardinia
Naples
Otranto
Athens
Smyrna
Al Ushbunah
Qurtubah (Córdova)
Cartagena
Panormus
Sicily
Calabria
Mediterranean Sea
Caliphate of Bagdad
Catania
Crete
IDRISIDS
RUSTAMIDS
ABBASIDS (AGHLABIDS)

FIRE AND SWORD

The relative peace and security established during the rule of the Carolingians ensured that most of western and east-central Europe was protected from attack. The spread of Christianity under the impetus of missionaries from Ireland and the enforced conversion at the point of the sword in places like Saxony aided the growth of churches and religious communities. Their wealth added to that of merchant settlements proved an attractive target to attacks from three marauding groups: Muslims from North Africa, Vikings and Magyars. The Muslim raids were a continuation of Islamic conquest. Sicily was occupied by 827, the victorious Aghlabids from Tunisia moving into the Balearics, attacking Sardinia and Corsica and establishing bases in southern Italy. One group, from either the emirate of Córdoba or Tunis, used Fraxinetum in Provence as a permanent base to penetrate southern Europe. Overall, the Muslims robbed, ransomed or raided Italian monasteries and towns, including Rome, and the Aghlabid fleet reigned supreme in the central Mediterranean. Further expansion was prevented by the Byzantine empire's reviving its fleet and reducing the Italian bases, together with the disintegration into civil war in the Muslim states of Spain and North Africa. In the the east, Arabs captured Crete, keeping it from 827 to 861, and shared control of Cyprus. Arabs plundered Thessalonica (904) and defeated a Byzantine expedition to Crete (911).

The Magyars comprised a different type of threat. Arriving in the Danube Plains in the 890s, these nomadic horsemen raided with extreme mobility and speed, plundering in turn northern Italy, Germany and France (c. 899–955) and terrorizing as far afield as Constantinople. Difficult to combat, the Magyars were rarely vulnerable except in mountains and at river crossings. The Saxon emperor Henry I defeated them at Riade (933) in Thuringia, while his son, Otto I, crushed them at Lechfeld in 955. Thereafter, the Magyars, under Geza and Stephen I, becoming Christians, settled what was to become a strong Hungarian state. The Vikings possessed seaborne mobility, descending on unsuspecting coastlines and sailing up rivers. Although Viking activity appeared essentially violent, these raiders could also be colonists. Bases were established in Ireland (Dublin, 841) by Norwegians who ravished Ireland and parts of Britain; Danish Vikings settled what became known as the Danelaw in England and settled Normandy in France. Vikings penetrated the Mediterranean, while others colonized the Orkneys, Shetlands, Faroes and Iceland, and reached Greenland and the Americas. Swedish Vikings crossed the Baltic and sailed down the Dvina-Dnieper complex to the Black Sea, while others reached the Volga and Caspian Sea. Establishing colonies at Novgorod and Kiev, these Varangians challenged Khazar control of the Constantinople–Black Sea trade. Eventually, they founded the Kievan Rus state but were absorbed by the Slavs and subjected to Orthodox Christianity. By 1000, the Magyar, Muslim and Viking scourges had practically ceased. However, the raids and conquests had two major results. First, the far-flung Viking network established new interlocking trade routes, and second, the weaknesses shown by Frankish and Byzantine leadership saw a devolution of power to local lords for defense purposes, leading to the rise of feudalism.

FIRE AND SWORD, c. 910

→ Viking invasions

➡ Magyar invasions

→ Abbasids invasions

▨ permanent Scandinavian settlement

Arctic Circle

Norwegian Sea

FINNIC PEOPLES

NORWAY

Hladir

Kaupang

SWEDEN

Uppsala

Birka

Baltic Sea

Staraya Ladoga (Aldeigjuborg)

Novgorod (Holmgard)

KIEVAN RUS

North Sea

DENMARK

Lund

Roskilde

Hedeby

BALTIC PEOPLES

KINGDOM OF ORKNEY

IRISH KINGDOMS

Dublin

Cork

WELSH STATES

NORTHUMBERLAND

York

WESSEX

London

Bremen

R. Rhine

Aachen

Cologne

Frankfurt

SLAVS

Kiev

Cracow

Bayeux

Paris

Orléans

EAST FRANKISH KINGDOM (GERMANY)

Lorch

Nitrava

HUNGARY

Mosapurc

ATLANTIC OCEAN

WEST FRANKISH KINGDOM (FRANCE)

Besançon

UPPER BURGUNDY

Lyon

LOWER BURGUNDY

Milan

Genoa

Venice

CROATIA

Serbia

Nish

PECHENEGS

R. Danube

Presov

Constantinople

BULGARIA

Bordeaux

Bayonne

NAVARRE

ARAGON

Avignon

Nice

Fraxinelum

KINGDOM OF ITALY

Adriatic Sea

Philippopolis

Adrianople

Corunna

LEÓN

Oporto

MUSLIM STATES

Barcelona

Tarragona

Corsica

Rome

Barium

Thessalonica

Toledo

Balansiyah

EMIRATE OF CÓRDOBA

Balearic Is.

Sardinia

Naples

Pr. of Benevento

BYZANTINE EMPIRE

Aegean Sea

Smyrna

Ishbiliyah

Ibn Hafsun (autonomous)

Cartagena

Mediterranean

Panormus

Sicily

Thessalonica

Sétif

Tunis

Malta

Crete

Chandax

Sea

IDRISIDS

RUSTAMIDS

ABBASIDS (AGHLABIDS)

Kairawan

Tripoli

69

EMPIRE AND PAPACY

The German conquest of Italy in the tenth century and the acquisition of the imperial title demonstrate that of all the lands of Europe, Germany had recovered first from the anarchy of the late Carolingian period and that the Saxon kings Henry II "The Fowler" (918–936) and his son Otto I "The Great" (936–973) were the true successors to the Carolingian empire. Henry conquered Italy in a series of campaigns between 951 and 972, and was crowned as Holy Roman emperor in 962, by Pope John XII. Otto ordered that every pope should swear allegiance to the empire. Later his grandson Otto II (980–1002) even dreamed of establishing his government in Rome, in an attempt to return to the idealized glories of Roman *imperium*.

The Saxons and their successors, the Salian and Hohenstaufen dynasties, maintained imperial predominance by regaining control over the royal demesnes within each duchy and by breaking each duke's control over the church within his land. The transhumance court, continually on the move throughout the German lands and northern Italy, enabled the emperor to enforce his will even further and led to an increasingly closer relationship between the empire and the church, which became a pillar of the monarchy and an instrument of the crown.

In the meantime, a rift arose between emperor and pope over who had the ultimate God-given authority over western Christendom. Known as the Investiture Controversy, this centred upon the pope's right to invest or crown the emperor and the right of lay rulers to grant ecclesiastical officials the symbols of their authority. In 1059, in an attempt to extract the papacy from the control of the emperor, Pope Nicholas II had given orders that in future all papal elections should be carried out by the College of Cardinals. The Investiture Controversy really began in 1075, when Pope Gregory VII (1073–1085) claimed supreme legislative and judicial power within Christendom, with the right to depose any prince and excommunicated five of the emperor's officials. As a reaction, the emperor, Henry IV (1050–1106), supported by the northern Italian bishops, ordered the imperial bishops to excommunicate the pope; Gregory VII in turn excommunicated the emperor and declared him deposed. Subsequent rebellion by the German barons and the dwindling of his support, forced Henry to seek penitence by crossing the Alps in winter in 1077 at Canossa, where he stood barefoot and in rags for four days, begging the pope's forgiveness. Despite this, Gregory would be forced to excommunicate Henry again in 1080, leading to war between the empire and the papacy. Gregory appealed for help to Robert Guiscard, the Norman duke of Apulia and Calabria, who marched on Rome and rescued Gregory in 1085. In the meantime, Henry, backed once again by the German bishops, appointed Clement III as an "antipope" in Gregory's stead.

Pope Innocent III (1198–1216), building upon the earlier reforms, had an exalted view of the papacy in Christendom and increased both the power and prestige of the church and the papacy based upon the right of the pope to approve or reject elections to the imperial throne. Innocent III excommunicated Otto IV (1182–1218) for having invaded Sicily in 1210 and supported the election of Frederick II Barbarossa to the imperial throne in 1212. A truce between pope and emperor would be established later with the Concordat of Worms in 1122.

THE EMPIRE AND THE PAPACY

Baltic Sea

KINGDOM OF DENMARK

Prussia
1231 won by Teutonic knigts

North Sea

County of
Holstein ○ Lübeck
○ Oldenburg
• Mecklenburg
Hamburg
Lüneburg • Ratzeburg
Slavinia

Friesland
Bremen •
Verden •
March of
Havelberg
Brandenburg
Brandenburg

Duchy of
Saxony
Osnabrück ○
Minden •
Hildesheim •
Brunswick
Magdeburg

Duchy of Pomerania
1181 imperial fief

○ Gniezno

Utrecht ○
Nijmegen •
Detmold •
Halberstadt
Brabant
Paderborn •
Duchy of
Lausitz
1158 joined to Empire

KINGDOM OF POLAND

Duisburg •
Mühlhausen •
Merseburg •
Dortmund •
Naumburg •
Altenburg
Landgravate of Thuringia
March of
Meissen
Meissen •

Duchy of
Silesia
1163 imperial fief

Bruges •
Flanders
• Antwerp
Cologne ●
Aachen •
Remagen
KINGDOM OF GERMANY
Eger •
Prague ○

Opol
and
Ratibor
1163 imperial fief
○ Neisse

Hainault
Duchy of
Lower Lorraine
Liège
Oberwesel •

KINGDOM OF BOHEMIA
○ Olomouc
March of Moravia

Cambrai •
Trier •
Mainz ●
Gelnhausen •
Bamberg •

Reims •
Verdun •
Kaiserslautern •
Frankfurt
Würzburg •
Franconia
Worms •
• Nuremberg

Metz •
Trifels •
Speyer •
Heilbronn •
Weissenburg •
Esslingen •
Eichstätt •
Regensburg •
Duchy of
Austria
1156 imperial fief

Troyes •
Toul •
Strasbourg •
Hohenstaufen •
Freising •
Passau •
Duchy of Bavaria
• Linz
• Vienna
• Bratislava
Esztergom

Duchy of Upper Lorraine
Ulm •
Duchy of Swabia
Augsburg •
Munich •
Salzburg
Chiemsee
○ Budapest

KINGDOM
OF
FRANCE
Besançon •
Basle •
Constance •
Zurich •
Innsbruck •
Seckau •
KINGDOM
OF
HUNGARY

County of
Burgundy
Solothurn •
Bern •
Fribourg •
Chur ○
Gurk •
Lavant •
Graz •
Duchy of
Styria
Duchy of
Carinthia

Lausanne •
Disentis •
Brixen ○
Geneva •
Sitten •

Lyon •
Vienne •
Savoy
Aosta •
Como •
Bergamo •
Trent •
Patriarchate
of Aquileia
March of
Carniola
Aquileia
Treviso •
Vicenza •
Grado
Tarentaise •
Ivrea •
Milan ●
Brescia •
Verona •
Padua •

KINGDOM
OF
BURGUNDY
1033 joined to Empire
Valence •
Novara •
Turin •
Vercelli ■
Lodi •
Cremona ■
Mantua •
March of
Verona
• Venice

Die •
Viviers •
Embrun •
Asti •
Tortona ■
Piacenza ■
Parma ■
Ferrara •
• Comacchio

Saluzzo •
Alessandria ■
Modena ■
Bologna ■
Ravenna •
KINGDOM OF ITALY
Emilia
Romagna
Luna •
• Rimini

Avignon •
Digne •
Genoa •
Fano •
Arles •
Provence
• Nice
Pisa •
• Ancona
Aix •
Marseille •
Fréjus •
Florence •
March of Ancona

Toulon •
Siena •
Duchy of
Spoleto
Camerino •
Tuscany
Perugia ○
Spoleto •

Adriatic Sea

Mediterranean Sea

Corsica

Sutri •
Patrimony
of St Peter
Rome ●
Tivoli •
Anagni •

KINGDOM
OF SICILY
1194 conquered by Henry VI

N

Sardinia

0   100 km
0   100 miles

THE EMPIRE AND THE PAPACY

— Empire border, 1152

Kingdom of Germany

Kingdom of Italy

Kingdom of Burgundy

Kingdom of Bohemia

imperial land in Italy

Hohenstaufen demesne land

Welf demesne land

ecclesiastical land

● archidiocese

○ diocese

■ Lombard League town, 1167

THE CRUSADES

Pope Urban II at the Council of Clermont on 27 November, 1095, proclaiming the First Crusade and calling on the knights of christendom to liberate the Holy City of Jerusalem.

"In all the streets and squares of the city, mounds of heads, hands and feet were to be seen. People were walking quite openly over dead men and horses." *Raymond of Aguilers,* eyewitness of the capture of Jerusalem

The Crusades were a series of military expeditions, carried out between 1095 and 1270, with the essential, though not exclusive aim of freeing the Holy Land from Islam. In the eleventh century, Europe experienced a religious revival that stimulated the growing popularity of pilgrimages to the Holy Sites, which were controlled by the Muslim Seljuk Turks, who were also threatening the Byzantine empire.

It was against this background that the First Crusade was launched in 1095 by Pope Urban II at the Council of Clermont; it would serve as the prototype of the crusades that were to follow, the object being to assist the Byzantine empire in its struggle against the Seljuk Turks. Although armies were raised by knights, such as Bohemond, Hugh of Vermandois and Robert of Flanders, the First Crusade was as much a pilgrimage as a Holy War, with indulgences being offered to pilgrims on their journey toward the Holy Sepulchre. Antioch was taken by Bohemond in 1098, after a siege lasting many months, and Jerusalem fell to the Crusaders in July 1099; its Muslim and Jewish inhabitants were put to the sword. The kingdom of Jerusalem was founded by Baudoin in 1100, alongside a loose federation made up of the principality of Antioch and the counties of Edessa and Tripoli. These were defended by a line of "Crusader" castles along the Palestinian littoral.

The fall of Edessa to the Turks in 1144 resulted in the Second Crusade, led by Louis VII, king of France, and the emperor Conrad III. When their forces arrived in Syria, instead of retaking Edessa, they laid siege to Damascus in 1148, but failed to take it. The ensuing defeat froze relations between the Crusader states and Europe for decades.

With the fall of Jerusalem to Saladin in 1187, a Third Crusade was called by Pope Gregory VII and led by the kings of France and England, who travelled by sea, joining Frederick II, who had taken the land route. Cyprus was taken and Acre put to siege by Richard the Lion Heart; although he failed to capture Jerusalem and was obliged to treaty with Saladin in 1192, he secured access for European pilgrims to the Holy Sites for a period of five years.

The Fourth Crusade was launched by Pope Innocent III, retaking Egypt, but it was diverted when the Crusaders took the Hungarian town of Zara for the Venetians as recompense for their sea journey. When the Crusaders eventually arrived in Constantinople in 1204, they captured the Byzantine capital and in league with the Venetians founded the Latin empire, which lasted for sixty years and seriously weakened the Byzantine empire, thus ending any possible reconciliation between the Orthodox and Latin churches.

In 1215, the king of Hungary set out for Acre, launching the Fifth Crusade. In 1218, the king of Jerusalem, Jean de Brienne, invaded Egypt and put the port of

Damietta to siege; however, his subsequent march on Cairo ended in disaster in 1221.

The Sixth Crusade was launched in 1223 by Pope Honorius III in support of an expedition led by Emperor Frederick II, who would later be excommunicated for his procrastination. The Sultan eventually gave up Jerusalem, Bethlehem and Nazareth to Frederick and signed a ten-year truce in 1229.

The Seventh Crusade, originated in 1239, was led by the king of Navarre and the duke of Burgundy. Nevertheless, Jerusalem fell once again to Muslim forces. St. Louis then led a campaign against Egypt; he captured the town of Damietta in 1249 and marched on Cairo, captured in 1250.

Antioch fell in 1268, which resulted in an Eighth Crusade, led by the king of France, who attacked Tunis, but died during the siege in 1270, his army subsequently being forced into retreat.

There would be other Crusades, even into the fifteenth century, which tended to be more anarchic in character, the result of popular outbursts of enthusiasm.

THE CRUSADES

religion

Latin (Catholic) Christian

Greek (Orthodox) Christian

Armenian Christian

Muslim

route of crusades

First Crusade, 1094–99

Second Crusade, 1146–49

Third Crusade, 1189–92

Fourth Crusade, 1202–04

Fifth Crusade, 1228–29

Sixth Crusade, 1248–54

Seventh Crusade, 1228–29

Mongol invasion, 1240–41

battle

RUSSIA AND THE TATAR INVASIONS

"O brave and courageous Russian sons, try to defend your country Russian land, from the Tatars! Make all necessary sacrifices in order to put an end to the burning and pillaging of your homes, the killing of your children, the abusing of your wives and daughters."
Polnoe Sobranie Russkikh Letopisei

The Tatars (or Mongols), moving westward from the heart of Asia, had a huge impact upon the histories of both Russia and Europe. A nomadic, Turkic people, the Tatars lived in the general area of modern-day Mongolia. They were united by Temujin (Genghis Khan) whose grandson, Batu Khan, following up on an earlier reconnaissance in force, led a lightning winter campaign against the northern Russian principalities with a large force in 1237 and subjugated the Rus and their neighbours in the west. This was the only successful winter invasion of Russia in recorded history.

First they defeated the Volga Bulgars, moving on to Vladimir Suzdal and destroying its wealthy towns. In 1239, due to internecine princely disputes, the Rus princes failed to form a united front, enabling the Tatars to overrun southwest Rus. They sacked Kiev and hundreds of other settlements in the process. By 1240, all Rus resistance had virtually ceased, and the Tatars were able to turn their attentions on Poland and Hungary. Although the Tatar conquest of northern Rus was part of a larger scheme, the conquest of Europe, they were unable to penetrate Europe because of internal disputes following the death of the Great Khan Ogedei in 1241. Nevertheless the Mongol conquest of all of northern and central Asia and eastern Europe made a strong impression in western Europe and successive missions, such as that of John of Pian de Carpine who, in 1245, would set out to the Golden Horde in an attempt to convert them to Christianity, leaving us with rich descriptions of their travels.

The Tatar conquest of Rus forced many principalities to submit to the hegemony of the "Golden Horde" (The Great Mongol empire). Only Novgorod, Pskov, and several lesser principalities would escape the "Tatar yoke", which technically would last until 1480. Yet, although the Tatars eventually converted to Islam, they remained tolerant of other religions and allowed the Russians to pursue Orthodoxy and to maintain their association, along the "Water Road", with Constantinople and the Byzantine empire.

From their capital at Sarai, the Tatars held nine principalities in their power. Tribute was exacted from all inhabitants, irrespective of status and class. The leading cities, centres of culture, were destroyed. Yet the Tatars also initiated a population census and had a considerable impact upon the Russian language. They also influenced military developments, especially cavalry tactics, which along with discipline and strategic co-ordination explained their successes on the battlefield.

The Tatars eventually withdrew to the steppes, restricting their intervention in the interior of Rus to punitive expeditions and the collection of taxes. Their ultimate defeat did not end their influence; their invasion would deeply affect Russia's future political, social and economic development, particularly by cutting Rus off from the rest of Europe. They also left an indelible imprint upon Muscovite life and society; the seeds of the "Russian Question" still are very much in evidence today, whereby Russia moved from a collectivity of independent principalities to an absolutist autocracy and from a system of diffused landholdings to the concentration of land in the hands of an autocrat.

SWEDEN

Gulf of Bothnia

FINNS

REPUBLIC OF NOVGOROD

Vyatka

Lake Onega

Lake Ladoga

R. Onega

R. Pinega

Velikiy Ustiug

to Rostov

R. Dvina

Gulf of Finland

Tallinn
to Denmark

Narva

Baltic Sea

ORDER
OF THE
SWORD
BROTHERS

Riga

CURONIANS

LITHUANIANS

PRUSSIANS

MAZOVIA

LITTLE
POLAND

1241

VOLHYNIA

1241

1241

R. Dniester

GALICH

HUNGARY

R. Danube

BULGARIA

Varna

SERBIA

to Venice

LATIN

EMPIRE

(ROMANIA)

Constantinople

Pskov

Novgorod

Vologda

ROSTOV

Sit River
4 Mar. 1238

Yaroslavl

Rostov

VLADIMIR
SUZDAL

Torzhok

R. Volga

PEREYASLAVL

1238

Suzdal
Vladimir

YURIEV

Nizhniy
Novgorod

Kazan'

Polotsk

POLOTSK

SMOLENSK

Smolensk

Moscow

Bulgar

VOLGA
BULGARIA

1236

R. Niemen

Minsk

Kozelsk
1238

CHERNIGOV

Ryazan

MUROM
RYAZAN

1230

TUROV-PINSK

Pinsk

R. Pripyat

R. Desna

NOVGOROD
SEVERSK

1223

N

S

R. Ural

Dec. 1240
taken by Tatars
Kiev

KIEV

1240

PEREYASLAV

1238

R. Don

M

1239

R. Volga

C

U

R. Donets

A

R. Dnieper

Kalka River
31 May 1223

Tunai

1242

Sarai

Astrakhan

to Kiev

Kaffa

Sudak

to Venice

to Kiev

L

A

N

S

Caspian
Sea

Black Sea

1223

Trebizond

EMPIRE OF TREBIZOND

GEORGIA

Tbilisi

1221

EMPIRE OF NICAEA

RUM
(ICONIUM)

R. Eastern Euphrates

LESSER
ARMENIA

0   200 km

0   200 miles

RUSSIA AND THE TATAR INVASIONS

▨	Russian principalities
→	Tatar raids, 1223 and 1230
→	Tatar conquest, 1236–40
→	Tatar raids from Russia to the West, 1241–42
✕	battle

THE FALL OF CONSTANTINOPLE

"It was his purpose to make Constantinople the most powerful and self-sufficient city in all respects, enjoying its previous level of attainment in terms of power, wealth, reputation, sciences, arts and all other affairs and fine accomplishments and in the quality of the buildings and monuments set up for the public good."
Kritovoulos on Mehmet II's rebuilding of Constantinople

The capture of Constantinople by the Crusaders during the Fourth Crusade in 1204 led to the creation of the short-lived Latin empire, which in turn accelerated the economic and political decline of the Byzantine empire, in favour of the Venetians, who were keen to destroy their main commercial rival in the Mediterranean. By the time that the Byzantines re-established power in 1261, the Venetians and Genoese had begun to play a greater part in the political and economic life of the Byzantine empire.

By the fifteenth century, the empire, riven by civil war, was much reduced in territorial size, to the city of Constantinople itself and the adjacent province of Roumelia, the Aegean coast and a few cities in Asia Minor. Byzantium had become heavily dependent upon Italian merchant colonies, while much of its territory in the Balkans lay in the hands of the kingdoms of Bulgaria and Serbia. By the mid fourteenth century, Byzantium, a shadow of its former glory, could no longer defend itself. Its army had been reduced to several thousand men by the time that the Ottomans had begun making inroads into Thrace from Asia Minor.

In 1355, the Ottomans took possession of the Dardanelles, and during the 1370s, they captured Adrianople, Macedonia and northern Greece, decisively defeating the disunited Serbian armies, led by Prince Lazar, at the battle of Kosovo in 1389.

Constantinople was put to siege in 1422 by Sultan Murad, a siege that the Byzantines would endure until 29 May, 1453, when Sultan Mehmet II's troops stormed the city walls after a bombardment that lasted for a whole month. The city was pillaged and sacked, its citizens massacred, raped or put to flight. The great church, Hagia Sophia, was converted into a mosque. The Byzantine empire ceased to exist.

The fall of Constantinople enabled the Ottomans to dominate the straits and the southern shores of the Black Sea. They were now able to advance through the Balkans to the Pannonian Plain, where Hungary now became the main European power to confront the Ottoman expansion.

This fresco from Moldovita Monastery, Romania, shows the siege of Constantinople in 1453 by the Turks.

THE FALL OF CONSTANTINOPLE, 562–1430

extent of the Byzantine empire

565
814
1095
1328
1430

RECONQUEST AND UNIFICATION OF SPAIN

"Once you know that the Spanish Church is being continually worn down by such a succession of disasters and by so many deaths of the sons of God as a result of the oppression of the pagans, we believe that not one of you will lie low."
Pope Calixtus II, proclaiming a Crusade in Spain, 2 April, 1123

Weaknesses within the ruling family of the caliphate of Córdoba and internal clashes between various Berber and Arab factions fragmented Muslim Spain into a series of emirates. The tiny Christian kingdoms of Léon, Navarre, Aragon and the county of Barcelona eventually united into two states: Léon was linked with Castile in 1037 under Ferdinand I, while Aragon achieved union with Barcelona (Catalonia) in 1118. The recognition of its independence by the pope in 1179 strengthened Portugal against Léon's ambitions. The monarchs were aided in their efforts by orders of knights that were established to fight the Muslims. A major Arab defeat in 1212 at Los Navas de Tolosa led to rapid capture of Córdoba (1236), Valencia by Aragon (1238), Murcia (1243), Seville (1248), Cádiz (1262) and the Algarve by Portugal (1250). Castile now controlled over half of the Iberian Peninsula, hemming in Portugal to the west and Aragon to the east. Granada remained the last Arab state in Spain and enjoyed a period of cultural brilliance under the Nasrid dynasty that endured until 1492. Portugal and Aragon channelled their energies elsewhere. Using the seapower of the Caláns, Aragon captured the Balearic Islands (1228) and seized Sicily (1282) and Sardinia was incorporated in 1320. Aragonese power reached its apogee in 1442, when Alfonso V conquered the kingdom of Naples. The Portuguese experience was different. Diniz, the "Farmer King", encouraged agriculture, aided by Cistercian skill; founded the first Portuguese university at Coimbra; and was responsible for the development of a navy. In 1294, he signed a commercial treaty with England to which Portugal permanently allied itself by the Treaty of Windsor (1386).

The impact of the reconquest was felt in other areas. The centralization of church influence was seen in the economic exploitation of Jews, the infringement of rights of converted Moors (Moriscos) and the growth of the Inquisition. The crown took over the orders of knights, lest they become too rich and powerful. The country became extremely religious, the process being accelerated by the marriage of the Catholic monarchs, Isabella of Castile and Ferdinand II of Aragon (1469). The conquest of Granada in 1492 saw the expulsion of Jews and

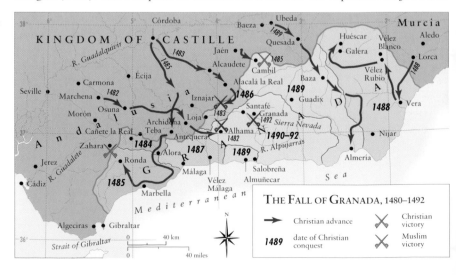

THE FALL OF GRANADA, 1480–1492

→ Christian advance
✕ Christian victory
1489 date of Christian conquest
✕ Muslim victory

Moriscos in a bout of religious intolerance. Despite the excesses of the reconquest and unification, the impact of Muslim culture can be seen in the Alhambra, architecture and garden design, and also in the influence of Arab mathematics, medicine, philosophy, and the study of Latin classics.

The Ties of Trade

The expansion of the western European economy maintained itself during the medieval period until curtailed by the Black Death. Before this slump, developments in shipbuilding (the Hansa cog), the opening up the Baltic hinterland by the Teutonic knights, a newly awakened European demand for Middle Eastern goods and the growth of the Genoese and Venetian trading fleets, all allowed a web of trade routes to penetrate Europe and link together areas of textile production, with markets being established in fairs such as that at Antwerp, which became the mercantile metropolis of western Europe. In the Baltic, German merchants established a union between Lübeck and Hamburg, and in 1252 they signed advantageous commercial treaties with Flanders (Bruges). An alliance was made, eventually numbering eighty-five members. Known as the Hanseatic League, its mercantile interests obtained full or partial control of trade between Germany and the coastal towns of eastern England. Although the members sought to destroy piracy and foster safe navigational techniques, they established trading bases, monopolies and commercial enclaves (kontore) in foreign towns such as Bergen in Norway, the Steelyard in London and Novgorod in Russia. This protectionist policy aroused considerable opposition and occasional warfare with rival towns. The goods traded were rich and varied including textiles, metals, salt, fish, grain, wine and luxury items. The league's strength was eventually reduced by the growing power of non-German Baltic states: the Union of Kalmar between the Scandinavian kingdoms (1397) and that between Lithuania and Poland (1386), together with the rise of Muscovy.

An illustration from the Hamburg City Charter of 1497, reflecting the seaport and its trades. In 1510 Emperor Maximilian I made Hamburg a free imperial city.

Trade in the Mediterranean benefited from the gradual ebb of Arab power. The Spanish Reconquista, the Crusades and the Pisan-Genoan liberation of Corsica and Sardinia left trade falling into the hands of the city-republics of Genoa, Venice and Pisa. Genoa and Venice grew wealthy and powerful with the carrier business during the Crusades and grew knowledgeable about the Levant. Chief items of trade were oriental silks, brocades and other textiles, ivory, perfumes and especially spices; these were exchanged for wool and other European goods from the network of cities in northern Italy, Germany and Flanders. Genoese forts and trading posts spread through the eastern Mediterranean, the Aegean and the Black Sea, causing intense rivalry with the growing enterprise of Venice. In 1284, a victorious war with Pisa brought Genoa the islands of Corsica, Elba and Sardinia (until 1326). Genoa was internally weakened by bitter rivalry between competing families. A final blow occurred in 1380, when the Genoese fleet fell into Venetian hands, and the city became dependent thereafter on France or Milan. Venice then became the most important naval and trading power, partly due to its geographical position between the Alpine passes and Byzantium and to its port and fleet of galleys. During the Fourth Crusade, Doge Enrico Dandolo managed to secure a commercial empire when Venice and the Crusaders partitioned Byzantium. This empire included Crete and parts of Euboea, with sundry forts and trading posts on the Greek mainland. Control of the Dalmatian coast through Ragusa and occasional rule over Corfu ensured a thriving trade, as did the acquisition of Cyprus.

THE TIES OF TRADE, c. 1300

- trading area of Hansa
- Hanseatic route
- trading area of Genoa
- Genoese route
- trading area of Venice
- Venecians route
- town with commercial link with Antwerp
- silk production
- wool production
- textile production

PART V: NEW DIRECTIONS

The period between the late fifteenth century and the middle of the seventeenth century witnessed a number of new directions in European culture, politics and society. The main themes in this period were the development and spread of humanist thought; reform theology; scientific discovery; and overseas exploration. Although this period has traditionally been interpreted as one of great change, it had much that was in common with the late medieval world, whereby magic, astrology, miracles, witchcraft and superstition prevailed in the thoughts and beliefs of many people against a background of the harshness of winter, vagrancy, plague, famine, disease and the ravages of war with their attendant scourges of pillage, rape, torture and destitution. A man or woman could be hanged, burned or broken on the rack or wheel for giving voice to heretical ideas.

The key issues confronting people in the late fifteenth century revolved around faith, superstition, witchcraft and the Devil. Everything revolved around the idea of a life after death. How could one avoid purgatory and the eternal fires of hell? There was an interaction between religion, magic, alchemy and the rise of technical and scientific methods and discovery.

The Renaissance and Reformation were both a reaction against the authority and control of a corrupt church and a superstitious society, aided by the rise of the cities and an increase in trade and technical progress — a scientific revolution that presaged the eighteenth-century Enlightenment.

The whole issue of Reformation and Counter-Reformation has to be put into the context of being a movement, almost a revolution, that kicked against all accepted doctrine, ideas and belief systems in Europe at the time. The Reformation was primarily a religious dispute that took place at a time when religion totally occupied people's lives. Nobody in society could escape from religion, which was an all-pervasive phenomenon that permeated every level of society. Yet although a religious dispute in its origins, the Reformation was soon hijacked by politics and more worldly issues.

The structure of European society at the time that the medieval world was "waning" (to paraphrase Huizinga) was portrayed as a transcendental hierarchy that descended from God, to his angels, to the pope, the Holy Roman emperor, the kings, their queens, the princes, lords and ladies, merchants and seamen, down to the serf or peasant cultivating his master's land. Nevertheless, if we look more closely at some of the secular art at the beginning of the sixteenth century, we might perceive how the times were changing. The artist Holbein, for example, in a series of woodcut prints entitled *Dance of Death*, illustrated a new mood. Despite the hierarchy in society, from pope to peasant and prince to beggar, one thing linked them all: death — death the leveller; with the portrayal of death, enticing prince, beggar and the common man. But where to: Heaven, Purgatory or Hell? If life as experienced on earth was transmogrified into a long and weary vale of tears, deeper thought was given to the afterlife, which could be the individual human being's recompense for so much earthly suffering. This problem of securing a place in Heaven, through piety and good works, or by buying a papal indulgence to expiate one's sins, lay at the heart of religious and social life, which

"The papacy is not other than the ghost of the deceased Roman empire, sitting crowned upon the grave thereof."
Thomas Hobbes
Leviathan

would result in strife for more than a century, a strife that would not really end until the Treaty of Westphalia of 1648, bringing to an end the bloody and destructive Thirty Years' War.

Toward the end of the Middle Ages, the church had been in a state of crisis. It was rotten from top to bottom. There had been the fourteenth-century crisis of the Avignon captivity of the pope, followed by the Great Schism, when there were two, even three rival popes. After the Council of Constance (1414–1418), the bishops struggled with the pope to turn the church into a limited, instead of an absolute monarchy. Spiritually there was corruption and venality. A succession of popes in the fifteenth century and the early sixteenth century failed to reform.

Could the church have reformed itself without a schism? The very fact that Pope Paul III was obliged to call the Council of Trent in December 1545 highlighted the need for the so-called Counter-Reformation, or Catholic response to the Reformation and was an admission by the church that reform was needed from within. The Council of Trent defined doctrines, introduced ecclesiastic discipline and reformed abuses within the Catholic Church, while strengthening the authority of the pope. The problem for the Catholic Church was that Pope Paul III (1534–1549) was acting twenty-eight years too late. The reforms that came were too late to alter the course of schism within western Christendom.

In the meantime, in 1534, a new religious order, known as the Society of Jesus, or the Jesuits, was founded by Ignatius Loyala (1491–1556); the Jesuits both reinvigorated Catholic Europe and won back many areas that had gone over to Protestantism. The Jesuits spread education and led missions to the "New World", converting the indigenous non-Christian populations of the Americas, Africa and Asia. In the meantime, the Inquisition, originally founded in Spain in 1478, had been reactivated by Pope Paul III in 1547, with the intention of extirpating heresy.

The Reformation took place at a time when the princes of the Holy Roman empire were consolidating their own territories in a process that established the modern principality and witnessed the decline of the feudal system.

A tremendous amount of power was consolidated in the princes' hands. They acquired territory through marriage, conquest or the exchange of distant territories. Crucial to this were developments in the judicial and financial systems, so that instead of being able to appeal to a wider authority, external to the principality, members of the clergy or nobility who went before the courts were obliged to appeal to their own prince. This increased the prestige of the prince, whose wealth grew through a more efficient system of tax collection and the ending of tax exemptions and local privileges.

The end of the fifteenth and the beginning of the sixteenth centuries were also a great period for the founding of universities. Seventeen had been founded in Germany in the space of a century. The German lands had a better record for university building than any other part of Europe. This was because every local prince wanted a university in his city. The universities attracted scholars and teachers at a time when there was a tradition of the wandering scholar who would

Henry VIII, king of England from 1509 to 1547, is mostly remembered for marrying six wives in a determined attempt to provide for the succession. The pope had refused to recognize Henry's original divorce from his first wife. This led after 1532 to a total break with the papacy and Henry declaring himself head of the Church of England.

move from one university to another, spreading the latest knowledge.

Hand in hand with the expansion of universities was the German Renaissance and the rise of Humanism. Humanism was a new attitude, a new intellectual movement, which from an intellectual standpoint witnessed the move away from the medieval world and medieval scholasticism and would become the basis of the western European education system well into the nineteenth century. Without the Humanists it is argued that there could have been no reformation. Desiderius Erasmus (1466–1536), Sir Thomas More (1478–1535), Ulrich von Hutten (1488–1523) and Philipp Melanchton (1497–1560) are typical examples of the new school of Humanism and many historical works repeat the old formula that "Erasmus laid the egg that Luther hatched".

Humanism and its pietistic Christian version, the *devotio moderna*, was an intellectual movement that flourished in advanced urban centres. The new city-states and university towns, the wealthy commercial centres and ports, such as Rotterdam and Antwerp, that were part of the new northward shift in trade and commerce from the Mediterranean provide the backdrop to the development of a "German" or northern Renaissance in opposition to its Italian counterpart.

Humanists were scholars who studied and taught the humanities — grammar, rhetoric, history, poetry and moral philosophy. Humanism was man-centred rather than God-centred. The work of the humanists was based upon writings and studies in Latin, and to a lesser extent in Greek, concomitant with the discoveries, rediscoveries and new developments of the Renaissance.

The humanists used the works of Latin and Greek authors, emphasizing the role of the individual and the individual conscience, essential prerequisites to the coming Reformation. A key theme to their work was a belief in the dignity and nobility of man. This was summed up in the words of Shakespeare's Hamlet, written at the end of the sixteenth century: "What a piece of work is man! How noble in reason! How infinite in faculty! In form, in moving, how express and admirable! In action how like an angel! In apprehension how like a god!"

There was a further break with medieval scholasticism, with a movement away from the contemplative life toward a life of action. Rather than spend their lives in monastic libraries and cells in deep religious contemplation, they moved toward an involvement in diplomacy, legal work and producing works on political theory.

That man could master his environment, independent of outside authority and as a complete individual in his thirst for all knowledge, was something of a progressive phenomenon in the mentality of the age as it tried to break free from the mental strictures of the Middle Ages. Yet ironically the Renaissance looked backward as it moved forward: back to the ideals of the classical age of Greece and Rome. It had started in Italy and spread out, but hardly touched those territories of Europe that had been occupied by the Ottoman empire or Moscow, once again widening the cleavage between east and west.

Likewise, from a religious point of view, there was a move away from the abstractions of theology, and its attendant superstitions such as indulgences, relics and pilgrimages, toward the problems of leading a good Christian daily life, where man's faith and his knowledge and understanding of theology should be based upon the authority of the scriptures and a direct relationship with God, through Christ. There was, with Humanism, a new belief that the individual now had a direct relationship with God, based upon faith and that there was no need to have a priest who acted as intermediary in worship and confession. These ideas were crucial to the Reformation.

Perhaps the greatest innovation in the late fifteenth century was that of printing. Printing provided the means of spreading the new religious, political, philosophical and technical ideas by reaching a wider audience. Printing has been described by G. R. Elton as a "new weapon". Without printing there would have been no Reformation, a limited spread of Humanism, and certainly a delay in technical and scientific transformation. Thirty years after Luther, professor of theology, had nailed his ninety-five theses (or arguments) to the church door at Wittenberg, printing presses had helped spread the ideas of the Catholic Counter-Reformation, so that all camps, political, cultural, religious and intellectual, would gain from its services.

The period was not only one of self-discovery through a different view of the position and role of mankind that initiated access to confessional difference, but also a period of the discovery of new lands — new worlds. The great voyages of discovery by Cabot, Columbus, Magellan, Vespucci and others posed navigational problems that acted as a further stimulus to scientific progress. In turn, the development of "Europe overseas" was only made possible by improvements in shipbuilding techniques. Improved compasses allowed for dead-reckoning in navigation. The work of astronomers made it possible to calculate accurately the latitude of vessels at sea — the problem of longitude, based upon accurate chronometers, would not be solved until the eighteenth century. One of the biggest bonuses to navigation was an improvement in cartography, of which Mercator's chart of 1569 allowed for the curvature of the earth, making it possible to plot a course at sea by drawing straight lines between two points.

The scientific revolution arose from the growing self-confidence, individualism and rediscovery of ancient texts that had all been stimulated by Renaissance Humanism, the logic of Protestant ideas and the rise of capitalism alongside the rise of urbanism and the changing social conditions of the sixteenth and first half of the seventeenth century. The spirit of scientific inquiry was afoot, based upon evidence and the realization that man's view of the universe and his place in it had been completely reshaped. The key areas of development were in navigation, which stimulated the exploration and conquest of the Americas and the development of trade routes to India; astronomy, through the discoveries of Nicolas Copernicus (1473–1543) and Galileo (1564–1642); mathematics, logic and physics through the works of René Descartes (1596–1650), Blaise Pascal (1623–1662) and Benedict Spinoza (1632–1677); all of these developments paved the way for the Enlightenment. By the middle of the seventeenth century, educated Europeans were living in a different mental world from their counterparts at the beginning of the sixteenth century.

OTTOMAN THREAT

The continuous struggle between Islam and the Byzantine empire, with interventions by western Crusaders, changed in emphasis during the fourteenth century, following the unification of Turkic tribes under able leaders from the Osmanli dynasty.

The Dardanelles were captured in 1355, when Osman's son, Orkham, landed in Gallipoli. Thrace was overrun and in the 1370s, Adrianople, the northern part of Greece and Macedonia were occupied. The Serbian nobility, led by Prince Lazar, were heavily defeated at the battle of Kosovo in June 1389, and by the end of May 1453, Constantinople fell to Sultan Mehmet II.

Now based upon the "Sublime Porte" at Constantinople, the Ottoman empire gradually spread through the Balkans and into the Pannonian Plain of Hungary. The Hungarians were defeated at the battle of Mohacs in 1526, and by 1529 Sultan Suleiman II attacked Vienna with an army of 250,000 men, although the Ottoman armies were obliged to abandon the siege after three days of violent fighting, withdrawing into Hungary and Romania.

The whole of the Balkans fell under Ottoman control until the nineteenth century. Croats and Serbs (the Prekocani), exiled north of the Rivers Sava and Danube, would act as frontier troops protecting Christendom and the Holy Roman empire from further Ottoman incursions.

In turn, during the next hundred years, the Austrians and Hungarians gradually drove the Ottomans back, although in the 1670s, the Ottomans struck back putting Vienna to siege in 1683, only to be driven off by Polish troops.

Ottoman success was not just predicated upon military prowess and organization, but also upon Ottoman diplomacy and a policy of tolerance toward non-Muslims, whereby Christian princes and nobles, such as Vlad Tepes of Transylvania or Marko Kraljevic of Serbia, were employed in the Ottoman service because they feared the potential spread of Habsburg power more than that of the Ottomans. Likewise, the Sublime Porte developed trade with the peoples around the Mediterranean coast, taking over from the Merchants of Marseille, Venice and Dubrovnik (Ragusa).

In this 17th century illustration, the Ottoman army reaches the gates of Vienna in 1683; meanwhile the Christian states had temporarily set aside their individual interests and in 1684 formed a Holy League under papal sponsorship.

OTTOMAN THREAT, 1328–1672

- Ottoman territory, 1328
- Ottoman territory, 1355
- Ottoman vassal from 1394
- Ottoman territory, 1402 (prior to Mongol attack)
- Ottoman territory, 1481 (Mohammed II)
- Ottoman vassal from 1475
- Ottoman territory, 1520 (Selim I)
- Ottoman vassal from 1541
- Ottoman territory, 1566 (Suleiman I)
- Ottoman territory, 1660
- Ottoman territory, 1630–72
- Ottoman vassal from 1664

PROTESTANT REFORMATION

"Hier stehe ich.
Ich kann nicht
anders. Gott
helfe mir.
Amen."
"Here I stand. I
can do no other.
God help me.
Amen."
Martin Luther,
18 April, 1521

The Protestant Reformation took place at a time of transition in the late fifteenth and sixteenth centuries. Change was fuelled by both a heightened religious awareness and the spread of the *devotio moderna;* and by the Renaissance, which boosted the interests of princely power and also led to greater intellectual curiosity, spread through humanism, whose key practitioners were Erasmus of Rotterdam and Sir Thomas More. In the background lay economic and social change engineered by a rising merchant and artisanal class and by the process of urbanization.

People began to question the role and nature of the Universal Church, which had grown corrupt and had become open to abuse and scandal.

Humanism demanded an improvement in scholarship and a break from non-biblical superstition and an independent-mindedness that underpinned the concept of personal salvation that, in terms of worship, did not demand the intermediary role of a priest between the individual and God. In the meantime, various lay social forces militated against an end to church taxation, for better standards of religious practice and duty. Anticlericalism came to a head in the German lands when Martin Luther, outraged by Cardinal Tetzel's sale of papal indulgences, nailed his ninety-five theses to the door of All Saints church in Wittenberg in October 1517.

The Reformation gave support to the rise of centralized and absolutist states with Luther, the Swiss reformer Huldrich Zwingli (1484–1531) and the Frenchman John Calvin (1509–1564) acting as the main proponents of reform against other forces, such as the Anabaptist and millenarian movements.

Anticlericalism and a hatred of church abuse was particularly strong in Germany. Politically the princes, imperial knights and city councils wanted to curtail the powers of the Holy Roman emperors Maximilian I and Charles V and the papacy. Church property was seized, and Protestant churches became subordinate to temporal rulers, a feature that would particularly benefit the monarchy in England, especially during the reign of Henry VIII.

In a failed attempt to unite the Protestant movement, Philip of Hesse tried to bring Luther and Zwingli together, where unity would only stumble upon their different interpretations of the Mass.

A new wave of Protestantism began with John Calvin, whose ideas spread from Geneva at the beginning of the 1540s into France, the Netherlands, the German lands and parts of eastern Europe, notably Poland and Transylvania.

Protestant political leaders formed the Schmalkaldic League in February 1531 in defence of Protestantism, and fought against Emperor Charles V in the war of 1546–1547. Charles V was never able to control the influence and spread of Protestantism in the Holy Roman empire, nor the political, economic and social forces behind it, since his hands were always tied by external demands: his wars with the French Valois dynasty, the Ottoman Turks and his need to control Spain and the Spanish Netherlands within the Holy Roman empire.

By the Treaty of Augsburg in September 1555, the decision was reached that subjects of each territory should follow the religion of the local prince according to the policy of *Cuius regio eius religio.* By this time, almost 40 per cent of Europeans accepted some version of "reformed" theology.

On this alter-front from Torslund in Denmark, a stronghold of the Protestant faith, Martin Luther, preaches to the converted.

The Protestant Reformation, c. 1560–72

- reformed faith dominant, c. 1560–72
- reformed faith growing, c. 1560–72
- considerable local reformed faith, c. 1560–72
- Catholic area
- seigneurial lands of the king of Navarre in France

- ■ Catholic mission and reform endeavours
- ■ reformed community discovered by the inquisition in Italy
- △ Papal nunciature, with date
- ⑥ number of legates sent to the last session of the Council of Trent,
- ✳ iconoclastic riots in Netherlands, 1566
- ✳ sectarian riots following the Saint Bartholomew massacre in Paris, 1572

HABSBURG RULE

The Netherlands, after refusing to carry the taxation demands of the Spanish crown, rose in revolt in 1568. The leaders of the revolt established the Union of Utrecht in 1579, which created the United Provinces. After a savage struggle, Dutch independence was eventually recognized in 1648.

"To God I speak Spanish, to women Italian, to men French, and to my horse — German."
Charles V, Holy Roman emperor (1519–58), king of Spain (1516–56) and founder of the Habsburg dynasty

A dynasty of German origins, the Habsburg monarchy ruled over a period of six centuries between 1278 and 1918. In 1278, Rudolph of Habsburg acquired the duchy of Austria and with time his family would become the leading dynasty in central Europe. In 1438, Albert of Habsburg, who had recently been crowned king of Hungary, was elected Holy Roman emperor, and that title would remain in his family's possession until 1806. In the fourteenth century the Habsburgs had gained Carinthia, Carniola, Tyrol, Istria and Trieste. As a single political entity the collection of territories that made up the Habsburg empire was a dynastic creation that would never be linked to one single nation, nor bound together by geography. The Habsburg empire would therefore become multinational in its make-up. Marriage, rather than conflict, gradually became the key to Habsburg expansion and through a series of marriages the dynasty acquired Burgundy in 1477, Bohemia in 1526 and Croatia in 1527. Throughout the sixteenth and seventeenth centuries the Habsburgs confronted two enemies: externally the threat of Ottoman Turkish expansion, while internally Habsburg power and authority were weakened by the rise of Protestantism. Whereas the Turks never managed to take the Habsburg capital of Vienna, despite the sieges of 1529 and 1683, the Protestant Reformation continued to undermine imperial power from within, culminating in the widespread chaos and destruction throughout much of central Europe during the Thirty Years' War (1618–1648).

Meanwhile in Spain Archduke Philip, son of Emperor Maximillian (1486–1519), had married Juana of Castile in 1496; they became king and queen of Castile in 1496. They were succeeded by their son Charles of Ghent, who became the ruler of the Netherlands on his father's death, then Charles I of Spain (1516 and 1556). Three years later in 1519, as Charles V, he was elected Holy Roman emperor, on the death of Emperor Maximillian.

Under Charles V, Burgundy was one of the richest imperial territories, ruled by his aunt Margaret of Austria between 1509 and 1530, and then by his sister, Mary of Hungary, between 1531 and 1555. Although Charles faced revolts in the Netherlands that were motivated by grievances over heavy imperial taxation, especially the revolt of 1539, worse would follow under his son and successor, Philip II (1555–1598), during whose reign there began an eighty-year-long conflict between 1566 and 1648, culminating in Dutch independence. Whereas Charles had mostly based his policy in the Low Countries upon a spirit of compromise, Philip made few concessions to Dutch local sentiments, privileges and confession. Worse, because he spoke neither French or Dutch and ruled from Madrid, the Dutch saw him as a Spanish king and therefore an alien, unlike his father, who had been born in the region.

In the meantime, under Cortés and Pizzaro the Americas had been conquered; yet despite the enormous wealth enjoyed by the Habsburgs from the Spanish Americas, all would be squandered on Charles's European projects and wars.

Charles's inheritance proved to be an impossible task; no sooner did one problem appear to have been resolved than another one arose. In Germany he had to confront the rise of princely power, posited upon the spread of the Protestant Reformation. He was constantly caught between the threats of the Protestants, the Turks and the French. In 1556 he abdicated; the Habsburg empire was divided into two, with his brother Ferdinand inheriting the Holy Roman empire and his son, Philip, inheriting Spain and its possessions in the Low Countries, the Italian lands and the Americas.

THE HABSBURG EMPIRE, c. 1600

- Spanish-Habsburg land
- Austrian-Habsburg land
- Habsburgs' traditional allies
- Habsburgs' enemies
- Church lands

— Holy Roman empire boundary, 1618

— 'Spanish Road', main supply routes to Habsburg possessions

→ route of Armada campaign against England, 1588

→ route of Spanish-Venetian fleet campaign against Ottoman empire, 1571

THIRTY YEARS' WAR, 1618–1648

THE THIRTY YEARS' WAR, 1618–48

- area of Bohemian War, 1618–20 and Palatinate War, 1621–23
- Protestant and Allied victory
- Emperor and the Catholic League victory
- area of Lower Saxon-Danish War, 1625–29 and Polish-Swedish War, 1625–29
- Emperor and the Catholic League victory

- area of Swedish War, 1630–34
- Gustavus Adolphus's main line of march
- Protestant and Allied victory
- Emperor and the Catholic League victory
- area of Franco-Swedish War, 1635–48
- Franco-Swedish victory
- Imperial and Allied victory
- indecisive outcome

This war, or series of wars, was perhaps the most costly seen in Europe, with great human suffering, pillaging and decline in population and trade, simultaneously with a general economic recession. The Thirty Years' War(s) served as the decisive phase in the struggle between Protestants and Catholics, which began in Bohemia in 1618 and spread to almost the whole European continent by the middle of the 1630s. The Thirty Years' War can be divided into five phases: the Bohemian War (1618–1620), in which the Imperial armies, under Tilly, invaded Bohemia from Austria and decisively defeated the Protestant Bohemian rebels at the battle of White Mountain in November 1620; the Palatinate War (1621–1623), with fighting to the west of the Rhine, in which Spain and the United Provinces (the Netherlands) renewed the Eighty Years' War, which had begun with the Revolt of the Netherlands in 1567; the Danish War (1624–1629), in which Tilly drove the Danes out of northwest Germany and Wallenstein occupied Pomerania and Mecklenburg, opening up the Baltic to the empire with the capture of the Hanseatic League ports of Wismar and Rostock; the Swedish War (1630–1635), when Gustav Adolf of Sweden, taking over the Protestant leadership

POPULATION CHANGE, 1618–48

estimated percentage of population decrease due to war and plague

66
33
15
no data

from Denmark and with Cardinal Richelieu's support from France, invaded Germany, destroyed Magdeburg and defeated Tilly at Breitenfeld and then Wallenstein in 1632 at Lützen (where Gustav Adolf was killed in battle); and finally the Franco-Habsburg War (1635–1648). Richelieu and his successor, Mazarin, in a risky strategy broke the Spanish encirclement of France and thus strengthened the French frontiers in coordination with the Dutch. With France's Swedish allies securing central and southern regions of the empire, the French largely concentrated on Spanish armies, culminating in the great victory at the Battle of Rocroi in the Ardennes in 1643, effectively ending Spain's military capabilities.

Peace negotiations began in 1638, ending in the Treaty of Westphalia (1648), which established the political frontiers of central Europe for over 100 years and the political and religious fragmentation of "Germany", thus preventing the emperor from turning "Germany" into an absolute monarchy based upon the principles of the Counter-Reformation. Some historians have seen in these wars a struggle that established a bipolar cleavage in Europe between two different cultures, the one characterized by the Counter-Reformation, absolutism, persecution and the Inquisition; the other by Protestantism, free institutions, civil society, religious toleration and the development of free-enterprise culture. This bipolar cleavage might well reflect perceived differences between east-central Europe and western Europe, which continue to impact on contemporary thinking and attitudes at the end of the second millennium.

EXPANSION OF RUSSIA

EXPANSION OF RUSSIA

- Russia, c. 1530
- Russian gains to 1613
- Russian losses to 1613

1584 date of conquest

● *1584* date of settlement

KIRGIZ peoples, tribe

→ unsuccessful military foray against Crimean Tatars, 1556–59

→ Yermack's route into Siberia, 1581–84

→ Crimean Tatar invasion, 1552–71

→ Polish and Lithuanian campaign in Livonian War, 1579–81

→ Ivan IV's campaign

Under Ivan IV, "The Terrible" (1533–1584), Muscovy developed into a centralized, autocratic state, building upon the achievement of Ivan III "The Great" and by weakening the power of the boyar aristocracy. From the beginning of the sixteenth century, Muscovy steadily began to increase pressure on the Tatar Kazan khanate and the Astrakhan khanate, bringing the bulk of the Volga Basin, as far as the Caspian Sea, under the control of Ivan by 1556. These victories opened the way to Siberia and the east.

Further expansion eastward would come in the early 1580s, when the Cossack Yermack conquered western Siberia. Meanwhile, with the establishment of a defensive line of fortresses centred on Tula, Ivan decided to go on the defensive against the Tatars in the east. He then turned his attentions westward to the Baltic, by attacking the Livonian knights in 1558 in an area equating with present-day Latvia and Estonia. This attack soon developed into a

Ivan IV "the Terrible" ruled Muscovy with a violent and sometimes unbalanced hand. His victims were not only members of the nobility but also members of his family, including his eldest son, whom he killed in a fit of rage.

major conflict with Denmark, Sweden, Poland and Lithuania, which would last for a quarter of a century. Ivan's initial successes turned to defeat when Poland gained most of Livonia in 1582, and Russia lost its territory in the Gulf of Finland and west of Lake Ladoga, including the cities of Yam, Kaporia and Karelia (Kexholm) to Sweden in 1585.

Whereas Russian expansion in the east had been successful, greatly expanding the size of Russia, Ivan's efforts in the west had turned to humiliating defeat. Access to the Baltic had been denied, nevertheless Russia was able to benefit from the discovery of a new route to the White Sea that had been opened up by English explorers and merchants in the 1550s. The port of Archangel was subsequently founded in 1584 on the mouth of the River Dvina.

On the death of Ivan IV in 1584, Boris Godunov acted as regent to Ivan's weak son Fyodor I, until the latter's death in 1598. Godunov continued to advance into Siberia, while waging a successful campaign in the northwest, thus winning back territory on the eastern Baltic coast, which Ivan had previously lost to Sweden during the Livonian War.

FRENCH DESIGNS

Louis XIV, king of France from 1643 to 1715. After 1661 he assumed absolute power, declaring "L'état c'est moi" "I am the state".

"Every time that I fill a high office, I make one hundred men discontented and one ungrateful." *Louis XIV,* known as the *Sun King*

Louis XIV symbolized the reassertion of royal power and divine right when he assumed power in 1661. The development of absolutism as an idealized political system coincided with the French struggle for European hegemony. However, any attempt at achieving ascendancy was predicated upon a reformed and strengthened France. The monarchy grew stronger by using royal agents *(intendants)* and the *Conseil du roi*, but at the expense of institutions traditionally checking royal power, the Estates-General and the Paris Parlement. The Gallicanization of the church, together with an assault on Jansenists and Huguenots, centralized religion, making the church a powerful instrument of state. The crown extended control over the economy through rules and regulations and Colbert's mercantilism. Académies (Académie Française), providing the environment for artists and writers like Poussin, Racine and Corneille, were established to promote standards in the arts and sciences. The army was reorganized by Le Tellier and Louvois. The new France was epitomized by the building of Versailles, an expression of power, might and authority. The centralizing absolution, combined with large natural resources and a population of twenty million, gave Louis XIV an excellent base for a carefully orchestrated foreign policy. His military objectives were limited and aimed at the security of France's frontiers. Weak borders, even protected by Vauban's fortresses, could readily be invaded through the Spanish Netherlands, Lorraine and from Italy. The thought that Habsburg possessions might be united (Spain and Austria encircling France) was a nightmare. Louis's foreign policy comprised various means: legal argument over the réunions to obtain Alsace, Lorraine, Flanders and Franche Comté; diplomacy resulting in the purchase of Dunkirk from England (1662); the use of subsidies to secure an alliance (1672 — Sweden against the Dutch); and aggressive combat in the War of Devolution, fought to successfully acquire several towns in the Spanish Netherlands and the Franche Comté in 1668, and that against the Dutch republic in 1672. The first ended in the Treaty of Aix-la-Chapelle, whereby Louis retained towns in the Spanish Netherlands such as Oudenarde, Courtrai and Ath; in 1670, France occupied Lorraine. The Franco-Dutch War engendered an anti-French coalition, including the Dutch, England, Austria, Spain and Brandenburg, which forced the Treaties of Nymwegen (1678). France lost certain towns in the north but finally won Franche Comté. By now, Louis had achieved more secure frontiers, and he was arguably at the height of his power. Two further wars dominated Louis's reign. The French seizure of Zweibruck and Strasbourg (réunions) occasioned the War of the League of Augsburg. This anti-French League was fought both in Europe and overseas colonies. The following Treaty of Ryswick (1697) compelled France to surrender most of her gains since 1678, but she retained Alsace and Strasbourg. The outbreak of the War of Spanish Succession (1702) again generated a large anti-French coalition. The Treaties of Utrecht (1713–1715) ended the long war, and France managed to acquire Barcelonnette, thereby securing her Italian border. Taken together, Louis's wars secured French frontiers, but their cost was enormous and a burden on the French people.

FRENCH DESIGNS

consolidation of French territory, c. 1460–c. 1560

- French territory, 1453
- annexed by France

1477 (1482) — date occupied (date confirmed)

— French border, 1559

○ parlement, with foundation date

France under Louis XIV

- - - administrative units created

defensive fortification built

→ possible invasion route

ENGLAND

R. Thames

English Channel

Flanders   Brabant

Dunkirk

Artois
1477–93
1526–29

Hainault   Namur   Limbourg

Picardy
1477 (1482)

Luxembourg

Cherbourg

Rouen
1515

Caen

Normandy

Reims

Lorraine

bishoprics
1552
(1559)

Alsace

Ile de Fance

Paris
1313

Chartres

Champagne

R. Seine

R. Marne

R. Meuse

Rennes
1492

Maine

Orléans

Troyes

Angers

Orléans

Franche-
Comté
1477–93

Besançon

Nantes

Anjou   Tours

R. Loire

Bourges

Dijon
1494

Berry

Burgundy
1477 (1482)

Poitou

Poitiers

R. Vienne

Bourbon
1527

R. Allier

Charolais
1477–93
1538–46

R. Saône

Gex
1536–59

La Marche
1527

Bresse
1536–59

La Rochelle

Forez
1527

Bugey
1536–59

Savoy
1536–59

Limoges

Clermont-
Ferrand

Lyon

R. Isère

Limousin

Auvergne
1527

Grenoble
1457

Bordeaux
1463

Dauphiné

Saluzzo
1548 (1559)

Turin
1539

Guyenne

Auvergne

R. Garonne

Languedoc

R. Rhône

Barcelonette

Gascony

Orange

Comtat
Venaissin

Provence
1481 (1481)

Avignon

Navarre

Toulouse
1451

Montpellier

Aix en Provence *1501*

Marseille

Toulon

Narbonne

N

SPAIN

Aragon

Cerdagne
1462–93

Roussillon
1462–93

Mediterranean Sea

Catalonia

0   50 km

0   50 miles

THE BALTIC BALANCE

After 1660, the Baltic region enjoyed an extended period of peace. Monarchs concentrated upon French ambitions and warfare and the conflict between Habsburgs and Ottomans. Sweden had achieved great power but now faced the problems of matching her limited economic and population resources with the responsibilities of governing and defending her recently acquired territories, thereby turning her into a "subsidy-hunting power". Russia was relatively backward and focused her foreign policy on the Black Sea, while Poland was weakened by the magnates' *liberum veto,* devastated by war, and intent on rebuilding the economy and developing her Baltic trade. Brandenburg-Prussia was to be drawn into French conflicts, while Denmark was internally reforming under an absolute monarchy and was too weak to confront Sweden. Nevertheless, all the old causes of resentment remained to be solved. Denmark sought to eradicate the threat of Holstein-Gottorp, the duchy straddling the south of Jutland that was allied to Sweden. Furthermore, Danish statesmen dreamed of regaining Scania to control the Sound and destroy Sweden's maritime hegemony. Brandenburg harboured jealousy of Swedish control of the River Oder in western Pomerania and resentment over loss of custom revenue from a 1653 treaty with Sweden. Brandenburg had designs on much of the Baltic littoral, Poland was eyeing Livonia, and ultimately Russian ambitions in the Gulf of Finland would conflict with Swedish interests.

In this situation, Sweden became dependent on French subsidies and was obliged to invade Brandenburg in 1675; her defeat at Fehrbellin by a force half her size was a severe blow to Sweden's military prestige and a portent for the future. When Denmark invaded Scania and defeated the Swedish Navy at Kjöge Bay (1677), Sweden was lucky to have Louis XIV intervene in the peace treaties, whereby Sweden kept all her empire, even western Pomerania, just captured by Brandenburg. Despite a number of vicissitudes in Swedish-Danish relations, Sweden managed to avert war, changed her political system into an absolute monarchy, and reformed the army, allowing her to defend her army without French subsidies, essential since Louis was now an ally of Denmark. By 1700, foreign affairs once again dominated the region, with Peter the Great of Russia seeking outlets in the Baltic and allying with Saxony/Poland, and Denmark against Sweden. Charles XII of Sweden began the Great Northern War with an attack on Denmark and then crushed the Russians at Narva. Despite his brilliance as a general, by 1713 the forces ranged against him proved too much. Onslaughts by Denmark, Russia, Prussia and Hannover were destroying the empire and Charles XII's death at Frederickshald in 1718 further weakened the Swedish position. Finally, British-French diplomacy helped achieve the peace treaties at Stockholm (Hannover, Prussia) and Nystadt (Russia). Hannover gained Bremen and Verden, Brandenburg won Further Pomerania and Russia received Karelia, Ingria, Livonia and Estonia. Russia was now the leading power in the Baltic but chose not to become dominant, having interests outside the Baltic. Franco-British interference was to ensure that there would be no successor power in the Baltic.

A Swedish ship sails into action against the combined fleets of Russia and Poland at the Battle of Oland, in the long struggle to dominate the Baltic.

SWEDEN'S BALTIC EMPIRE

- Sweden under Gustav Wasa, 1523–60
- Sweden acquisition, 1561–1645
- Swedish colonization in Finland
- iron ore
- ▲ copper
- ▲ silver
- ▲ gold
- sea frozen in Winter

ARCTIC OCEAN

North Cape

Kola

Kola Penninsula

Arctic Circle

Lofoten Is.

Kabelvåg

L a p p l a n d

White Sea

Norwegian Sea

Alstahaug

Västerbotten

Torneå

Luleå

Uleåborg

Österbotten

Carelia

Lake Onega

Trondheim
Trondheim

Angermanland

Umeå

S W E D I S H   E M P I R E

Nyslott

Jämtland

Herjedalen

Särna   Helsingland

Bjöneborg

Finland

Kexholm

Vyborg

Lake Ladoga

Falun

Nystad

Helsingfors

Ingria

Hamar
Christiania

Uppland

Åbo (Turku)

Ålaud Is.

Gulf of Finland

Narva

Novgorod

Bergen

Västerås

Uppsala

Reval

1561

1561

RUSSIAN

Christiansand

Bohuslän

Linköping

West
Gotland

East
Gotland

Visby

Dagö
1582

Estonia

1581

1581

Pskov

EMPIRE

Jonkoping

Gotland
1645

Baltic Sea

Windau
1621–29

Ösel
1645

Gulf of
Riga

Marienburg

Livonia

Riga

Courland

Libau

Jutland

Aarhus

Blekinge

Memel

Samogitia

Vitebsk

Smolensk

Copenhagen
Roskilde
Zeeland

Malmo
Scania

Bornholm
1658–60 to Sweden

Königsberg

Vilna

Orsha

Andrusovo

North
Sea

Kiel

Pomerania

Further
Pomerania

Danzig

Duchy
of
Prussia

Great Principality

of Lithuania

Minsk

DUTCH
REPUBLIC

Münster

Wismar
Mecklenburg

Lüneburg

Berlin
Brandenburg

Great Poland

Poznam

Kujavia

Mazovia

Warsaw

K I N G D O M   O F   P O L A N D

R. Bug

Polesia

Pinsk

Pripyet
Marshes

Norway

KINGDOM OF DANMARK AND NORWAY

Skaggerak

Gothenburg
Halland
1645

Kategat

Stockholm

Gulf of Bothnia

PART VI: THE IDEA OF STATE

The Battle of Edgehill in October 1642, during the English Civil War, was a seven-year struggle that culminated with the overthrow of the monarchy, completed by public execution of King Charles I in January 1649.

During the seventeenth, eighteenth and nineteenth centuries, the European peoples sought to construct modern states based upon more than a royal household and court. States developed into a broad spectrum of institutions — political, legal, military and administrative — to regulate society. These new states sometimes came to acknowledge or claim to represent their people politically. The inhabitants of each state developed their own explicit identities, which reduced or eliminated differences among them but distinguished them from peoples governed by other states. Societies were transformed economically by changing modes of production, maritime trade routes, and other means of distribution, leading to different concentrations of wealth. Institutions of state had to govern during these developments and were often influenced by diverse social classes or dominant elites. The historical formation of modern states was accompanied by a number of important processes. All states claimed to be democratic, even if they were not and most peoples attempted to broaden the political consensus and to limit arbitrary or absolute rule. Changing economic organizations developed the commercialization of agriculture and investment in capitalist endeavours, and the growth of industrial societies was eventually dominated by the factory system. States and the societies they governed felt themselves to possess a unique common identity based on cultural, linguistic, religious, historical or other factors, such as loyalty to a particular constitution. In sum, these were "nation-states" despite the existence of centrifugal ethnic groups such as Bretons in France, Basques in Spain and the chaos of east and central Europe. Governments also presided over societies showing a diversified class system, which could threaten national unity. Class was the pre-eminent socio-economic form in societies industrializing under capitalist economic conditions. Hence, class and class antagonism possessed major political importance. Assuming that the state favours the interest of one class above others, then dominated and exploited classes might seek change through democratic means or by violence. Socialist states have claimed to eradicate class divisions by acting in the interest of one class to destroy class differences. Hence, class conflict can result in events like the 1917 Russian Revolution or to a lesser extent, aspects of the 1789 French Revolution. Such events involve the state's exercising control on behalf of all people over the capitalist economy in order to socialize it. Therefore, all modern states are characterized by democratization, industrialization, nationalism, class tensions and socialism.

While most European states were moving toward the alleged centralized efficiency of absolutist monarchies, the system of estates of the realm or parliaments continued and developed in northwestern Europe, in the Low Countries and Great Britain. Both powers were great trading countries, the Low Countries taking first place. The rapid expansion of sea trade enriched enterprising citizens, both gentry and middle class, who were capable of playing a political role and defending their own interests, which often differed from the monarch or governing authorities. Several analysts have perceived a link between the Protestant Reformation and early capitalist industry and trade. R. H. Tawney in *Religion and the Rise of Capitalism* (1926) argued that individualism and the thrift of

Calvinist Protestantism nurtured industrial organization and an efficient work-force in northern Europe. He therefore moved and developed the ideas of Max Weber's *The Protestant Ethic and the Spirit of Capitalism*. This book argued that the ideological stage for the rise of capitalism had been prepared by Calvinist religious doctrines, especially predestination. Indeed, Weber thought that Roman Catholicism's hostility toward lending money for profit was contradicted by the Protestant conviction that wealth was a godly award bestowed upon the diligent and frugal. In the northern Low Countries, Protestantism took hold in areas resenting the fact that Roman Catholic Spain threatened traditional liberties. The Dutch Revolt protected local independence against central government, despite the dominant position of Holland among the seven provinces of the United Provinces. The new republic, whose existence was ratified by the 1648 Treaty of Westphalia, was an early form of liberalism and federalism. Legislative power was entrusted to each member province that appointed a jurist (pensionary) in charge of administration and a *stathouder*, the president of the province. Federal power was in the hands of the Estates-General, with delegates elected by the provincial estates. A Council of State controlled the army and exchequer. Mirroring local politics, a federal jurist (grand pensionary) and a *stathouder* were appointed. This situation was complicated by the grand pensionary, who was supported by leading merchants supporting autonomy for Holland confronting the *stathouder*, the prince of Orange, who had the backing of the lower classes, peasants and sailors, convinced Calvinists, who desired a firm, highly centralized state.

In Britain, tradition affirmed that the king was subject to the law, and he could not raise new taxes nor pass legislation without the consent of Parliament. When King Charles I, a convinced absolutist, confronted Parliament, imprisoned members and ruled for eleven years without Parliament, revolution was assured. In the subsequent civil war, fought in England, Scotland and Ireland, the king faced an alliance between a group of aristocrats and the prosperous middle classes. The latter were often innovating landlords, using experimental agricultural techniques and efficient business management, who were enclosing land and dispossessing small occupiers and cottagers, turning them into rural wage labour, the victims of agricultural capitalism. In the landlord's eyes, the king championed the old economic order, making him an obstacle to progress. Furthermore, support for the Roundheads, the Parliamentary Army, developed strongly among Calvinists and other dissenting sects, such as the Levellers. The Protestant faith was adopted by numerous middle class, artisan and merchant families who saw in the monarch, the personification of Roman Catholicism, an old enemy recalling Tudor wars with Spain. The king's defeat in 1647 and his execution by a legally elected legislature in 1649 ushered in a Cromwellian republican dictatorship (the Commonwealth), ironically ruling with a truncated Rump Parliament, all ending in 1660. This first revolution, together with example of the United Provinces, showed Europe the possibility of creating republics; this demonstration of anti-absolutist politics was ignored. The Restoration's attempt to return to absolutism under Charles II and James II failed, leading to the second Glorious Revolution, when important aristocrats invited William of Orange to invade England in order to preserve English liberties by ousting his father-in-law. William's military success was rewarded by Parliament, deciding that England should be ruled by William and Mary. The subsequent Bill of Rights embodied several principles, including: the power of law superseded that of the king, Parliament had to annually consent to levying taxes, and Parliament decided monarchical succession. Now Britain had a state based upon constitutional monarchy. The liberal political attitudes in Britain and the United Provinces provided the climate for producing leading anti-absolutist thinkers such as Hobbes, Locke and the Dutch jurist Grotius.

The 1789 French Revolution introduced a new type of state, producing a political earthquake, thereby undermining a Europe of absolutist states. A series of revolutionary ideas involving sovereignty of the people, republicanism and several versions of democracy were offered to Europe and the world, sometimes on the point of a bayonet. France demonstrated that the state should act in the interests of the people, the nation at large; that rule by inherited privilege and lineage was immoral; and that monarchy was evil and monarchs should be deposed, by violence if necessary. These novel ideas challenged dynastic rule and developments within the revolution confronted states with notions of direct democracy and egalitarian economic policies. By 1791, the French state was constitutional, republican, representative and essentially middle class. The Constitution included the separation of powers derived from Montesquieu's view of how the British constitution operated. Tom Paine, whose pamphlet *Common Sense* was so significant in the American War of Independence, became a member of the French legislature and wrote *The Rights of Man* (1791). This defence of the French Revolution became an analysis of discontent in Europe and a prescription for the sins of arbitrary government, including poverty, illiteracy, unemployment and war. The book included radical ideas demanding popular education, poor relief, old age pensions and public works for the unemployed. The original bourgeois Assembly eventually incorporated the *sans-culottes* (the urban poor) and was transformed into a direct democracy. Here, delegates to the Assembly were defined as mandate holders only and could be replaced at any time. Thus the *sans-culottes*, sought to extend forms of democratic control over the representative sate. The impact of war and the excesses of the Jacobin Committee of Public Safety led to a conservative counter-coup, with stability being organized by the Directory, a small oligarchy dependent on military support. Its incompetence and financial mismanagement opened the way for an autocratic military dictatorship, achieved by Napoleon's coup d'état in October 1799. The resultant attempt to conquer Europe was eventually ended at the battle of Waterloo in 1815.

After the ordeal of the Revolutionary and Napoleonic Wars, reason ordained that Europe would not return to the pre-1789 political and social status quo. A new means of keeping the peace through international arbitration was essential. Europe was to be reconstructed, based on the two principles of legitimacy and the balance of power. Legitimate sovereigns would have their lands returned and those remaining unclaimed — former republics (Genoa), free cities or church principalities — would be distributed to maintain the balance of power. These achievements made by the Congress of Vienna (1815) would be guaranteed by a Concert of Europe, whereby monarchs would meet regularly to discuss common interests and generate policies to solve common problems. Congresses were held at Aix-la-Chapelle (1818), Troppau (1820), Laibach (1821) and Verona (1822). Monarchs were interested in curbing revolutionary movements, whether liberal or nationalist. The power of conservative monarchs to restrain these new ideas resulted in major confrontations on city streets across Europe in 1848, after which rulers had to be more flexible in order to survive. Great Britain wisely extended the franchise over a number of years, constantly widening the political consensus but countries such as Russia and Austria-Hungary remained arch-conservatives. The tradition of congresses continued with the Congress of Paris (1856) ending the Crimean War and the Congress of Berlin (1878) concerning reorganization in the Balkans.

An unknown artist recorded this scene of unrest outside a factory gate in Vienna on 13 March, 1843, in the same year such events were repeated many times across Europe.

A major event of the mid nineteenth century was the exercise in German state-building. The series of wars creating the German empire (1871) was predicated upon an alliance between German industrial and commercial interests linked to the Prussian state bureaucracy and its military and agricultural aristocracy (the alliance of iron and rye). However, despite the Kaiser's retention of some remnants of absolutism, the state was constrained within an identifiable legal framework. This Rechtsstaat established a constitutional monarchy, even if it was not accountable to the elected representatives in the Reichstag. The nature of class and political alliances in Germany differed from other countries. The accommodation of Prussian absolutism with capitalist industrialization was confusing. The authoritarian and patriarchal legacy of Bismarck saw a Kaiser's state bestowing sickness, old age and disability insurance on a working class with its large Social Democratic Party, which also quite happily signed up for war in 1914.

Capitalist industrialization in Russia included an intense rural-urban drift where cheap and abundant labour fuelled an industrial revolution. Rapid industrialization and urbanization swelled a working class that suffered severe hardships. The impact of war on an inflexible and dysfunctional tsarist autocracy allowed Lenin and the Bolsheviks to manipulate the proletariat and establish a dictatorship of the working class (1917). However, this rapidly turned into a dictatorship by the party over the working class, eventually succumbing to Stalin's dictatorship over the party itself. In the aftermath of war, Lenin allowed a degree of economic freedom through the New Economic Policy, while consolidating political control over the country and by banning factionalism within the party. The surge toward monolithic and totalitarian power was noted, aided and abetted by Stalin who, as Commissar for Nationalities, carried out a bloodbath against his own Georgian people. Stalin's accession to power established a new style of dictatorship predicated upon economic planning, the purging of actual or potential dissidents, psychological terror and the gulags. However, the application of force in all policies allowed the Communists to expand industry to such an extent that the Soviet Union had the capacity to bear the major burden of the Nazi onslaught during the Second World War.

ENGLISH CIVIL WAR

Below centre: Cromwell at the head of his victorious cavalry after the battle of Marston Moor, in July 1644. Victory for the parliamentary forces seriously weakened the Royalist cause in northern England .

Against the background of science and reason that arose from the Renaissance and Reformation, the causes of the English Civil War were those of a growing hostility to the Stuart monarchy, embodied in the persons of Charles I and his French wife, Henrietta Maria. This hostility was based upon: constitutional resistance to absolutist monarchy, posited upon the principle of the "Divine Right of Kings"; resistance against centralism from county and urban radicals and borough representation in Parliament; and Puritanism and contempt for Laudism — High Church innovations that supported the privileges of monarchy and the principles of clerical authority over the laity. In the background there lay a general fear that England would return to Catholicism. Along with the intellectual stimulus of the Renaissance and Reformation, with a simultaneous growth in science and reason, was the spread of lay education in England, which resulted in the rise of an independent-minded and self-confident social group often influenced by the rise of English Puritanism.

The real issue was the rivalry between Parliament and the absolutist monarchy with the rise of the gentry and professional classes in a socio-economic revolution that was based upon social mobility, set against the weakening of the feudal aristocracy, the growth of capitalism in agriculture, trade and industry, and a general increase in population.

When Charles raised his standard at Nottingham in August 1642, the two opposing armies were more or less equal in number, although the Royalists were superior in cavalry until the formation of the New Model Army in 1645.

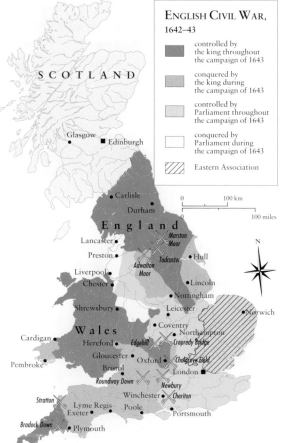

ENGLISH CIVIL WAR, 1642–43

- controlled by the king throughout the campaign of 1643
- conquered by the king during the campaign of 1643
- controlled by Parliament throughout the campaign of 1643
- conquered by Parliament during the campaign of 1643
- Eastern Association

The king's generals (Prince Rupert, Hopton and Newcastle) were less able than those of Parliament (Pym, Fairfax and Cromwell) in terms of organizational and fighting abilities. Furthermore with time the aristocratic officers began to quarrel among themselves.

Charles could successfully fight a short war, but as the war developed, Parliament began to win the upper hand, maintaining support and power in the richer and more populous southeast of England, especially in London, while Royalist support mostly came from the north and west of England and from Wales. Parliament therefore held access to the chief ports, the sea and the navy, thus maintaining an advantage over the Royalists, by maintaining an administrative centre in London, good communications and unified command. This position was enhanced by taxation, the availability of manpower and a constant supply of war materials. The key to parliamentary success was the religious, puritanical fervour, discipline, training and the development of a cavalry that became numerically superior with the creation of the disciplined and highly professional New Model Army.

The campaigns of 1642 brought small parliamentary gains in the northwest, but were countered by heavy losses in the southwest, so that it seemed certain that the king would win in 1643, until Parliament won the support of the Scottish Covenanters. Parliamentary victory at Marston Moor on 2 July, 1644, followed by the overwhelming victory by the New Model Army at Naseby on 14 June, 1645, ensured parliamentary success, although the war would continue for a further year and a half, with the king taking refuge with the Scots, only to be handed over as a prisoner of Parliament in January 1647.

The king would later escape from the army to the Isle of Wight, where he negotiated with the Scots, promising to establish Presbyterianism in England in return for their support. This led to the Second Civil War, more a series of royalist risings, backed by a Scottish invasion of England, which was repulsed by Cromwell. Charles was executed in January 1649.

The Third Civil War began in Ireland in 1649, when Cromwell suppressed a major rising of Catholics and Royalists at Drogheda and Wexford. Ireland was subjugated and a subsequent rising in Scotland was put down at Dunbar in September 1650 and utterly routed at Worcester in September 1651, which resulted in Charles II's flight abroad. A republic had been created whose power extended throughout the British Isles until the monarchy was restored in 1660.

> "You have sat too long here for any good you have been doing. Depart, I say, and let us have done with you. In the name of God, go!" *Cromwell*, dismissing Parliament, April 1653

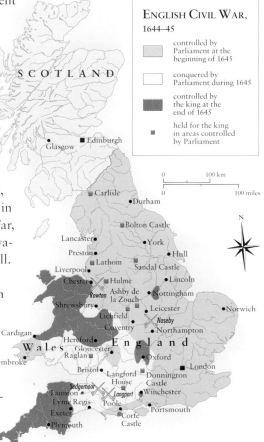

ENGLISH CIVIL WAR,
1644–45

controlled by Parliament at the beginning of 1645

conquered by Parliament during 1645

controlled by the king at the end of 1645

held for the king in areas controlled by Parliament

0   100 km
0   100 miles

SCOTLAND

Glasgow • Edinburgh

• Carlisle
• Durham
■ Bolton Castle
Lancaster •
Preston • • York
Liverpool • ■ Lathom • Hull
Chester • ■ Hulme Sandal Castle
Rowton Ashby de • Lincoln
Shrewsbury • la Zouch • Nottingham
Lichfield • Leicester • Norwich
Coventry Naseby
Cardigan Hereford • Northampton
Wales Gloucester • England
Raglan ■ • Oxford
Pembroke Bristol • • London
Langford Donnington
Sedgemoor House Castle
Taunton • Langport • Winchester
Lyme Regis Poole
Exeter • Corfe Portsmouth
• Plymouth Castle

REPUBLICS OF TRADE

"The prodigious increase of the Netherlands in their domestic and foreign trade, riches and multitude of shipping, is the envy of the present and may be the wonder of the future."
F. Charpentier, 1664

The Dutch revolt against Spain lasted from 1559 to 1648, but in effect Spain recognized the independence of the seven provinces in 1609. In a world of absolutist centralization, the Dutch republic emerged as a federation, each province retaining its sovereignty and local self-government and was unique, basing its wealth on commerce and industry rather than agriculture. The republic's government was aristocratic, but the separate provinces were suspicious of the House of Orange which provided necessary military leadership. Constant friction between *stathouder* and provinces resulted in a *stathouder*less period from 1650 to 1672. In a violent and insecure world, the republic soon came to blows with France (1672–1678 and 1689–1713) and England in three naval wars: 1652–1653, 1665–1667 and 1672–1674. Conflicts with England concerned trade after the English Commonwealth passed the 1651 Navigation Act, forbidding the Dutch from acting as transit merchants in English trade with Europe or overseas. During the final war, the Dutch gave full power to William III of Orange as *stathouder* to combat a Franco-British alliance. A major reason for Dutch survival was her trading interests, prosperity originally being dependent on links with the Baltic, France and the Iberian Peninsula.

The Dutch East Indies Company, constituted in 1602, established bases in India, Ceylon and Indonesia, the major trading centre being Batavia in Java. The European demand for spices and pepper allowed the monopolistic company to make huge profits when its fleet returned annually. Further wealth accrued from cessions of territory by native Javan Sultans and on the other side of the world the West India Company, founded in 1621, traded in commodities and slaves. Taken together, the Dutch cities became the major entrepôts of Europe, especially Amsterdam and Rotterdam, which handled about 50 per cent of world trade, while the Bourse at Antwerp was the centre of the European money market. So significant was the republic in European politics that three major peace treaties were signed on its soil: Nymwegen, Ryswick and Utrecht.

During this period, regarded as the Dutch Golden Age (1609–1713), a large measure of religious toleration allowed Calvinists, Lutherans, Roman Catholics, Anabaptists and Jews to coexist in a stability that encouraged trade and the arts. Ideas were readily debated, and Hugo Grotius became the progenitor of international law, while Spinoza found peace to investigate philosophy and science. However, the Golden Age is mainly remembered for its painting, resting upon local patronage. The Flemish School developed, with Rubens and Van Dyck painting landscapes and seascapes, while the Dutch School, including Frans Hals, Vermeer and Rembrandt, created portraits and group paintings. Architecture however, remained low key, except for the immense variety of roof gables.

The republic had relations with England other than war. In 1688, William II became king of England by virtue of his marriage to Mary II Stuart. Thereafter, Dutch internal affairs were managed by resident councillors and arguably this led to stagnation through competition with the English East India Company and the cost of war, especially with France.

THE NETHERLANDS, c. 1648

- Union of Utrecht, 1579
- Union of Arras, 1579
- joined Union of Utrecht by 1581
- United Netherlands, 1609
- to United Netherlands, 1648
- Spanish Netherlands, 1648
- boundary of Holy Roman empire
- border as at 1648

N

0 · 25 km
0 · 25 miles

Groningen
• Groningen

Friesland

Drenthe

R. Vecht

R. IJssel

Overijssel

Holland

Amsterdam

Zutphen

Leiden •

Gelderland

Utrecht

HOLY

• Rotterdam

Utrecht

R. Maas

R. Lippe

North

Zeeland

Sea

Lands of the Generality

Brabant

Upper Gelders

Mörs

R. Ruhr

Sluys

Antwerp

ROMAN

Brugge •

Ghent •

R. Schelde

Cologne •

Calais

Flanders

Brussels •

Maastricht •

Bishopric of Liège

Aachen •

R. Lys

Limburg

Lille •

Tournai •

Liège •

Artois

Namur

Arras •

EMPIRE

R. Sambre

Namur •

Hainaut

R. Somme

Luxembourg

R. Meuse

Trier •

R. Saar

FRANCE

R. Aisne

Luxembourg •

R. Oise

Reims •

Verdun •

Metz •

R. Marne

REVOLUTION IN FRANCE

This engraving by Carnavalet shows the execution of Louis XVI on 21 January, 1793.

"L'immoralité est la base du despotisme comme la vertu est l'essence de la République."
"Wickedness is the root of despotism as virtue is the essence of the republic."
Maximilien Robespierre, Revolutionary leader

The French Revolution of 1789–1799 would fuel the main political and social forces of the nineteenth century: democracy, liberalism, socialism and nationalism. It would result in a complete break with the feudal legal structure and the Ancien Régime.

Always open to controversial historical debate, causes of the French Revolution can be put down to demographic, economic and social change in the eighteenth century. The failure of wages to keep pace with price rises and a recession from the 1770s were exacerbated by poor harvests in 1787 and 1788. In February 1787 efforts to reform the financial system and remove the budget deficit introduced by the king's ministers Calonne and Necker backfired and resulted in further resistance from the aristocracy who, in 1788, in the hope of protecting their own rights, called for an Estates-General, made up of the three estates, Clergy, Nobility and the Third Estate, which met in Versailles for the first time since 1614.

Opposition from the middle-class representatives of the Third Estate would prove too strong, especially when they won the support of the Parish priests. Imbued by the ideas of the eighteenth-century *philosophes,* who advocated social and political reform, the Third Estate, led by Abbé Sièyes, established a National Assembly, La Constituante, on 20 June, in the Jeu de Paume tennis court at Versailles, and demanded constitutional reform. The formation of a Committee of Public Safety, the creation of a National Guard, and the symbolic fall of the Bastille on 14 July, turned revolt into revolution.

The subsequent Grande Peur, the great fear of unrest in the countryside, throughout the summer of 1789 led to revolutionary decrees, especially the Abolition of Feudalism and the Declaration of the Rights of Man.

Although the Revolution was not, in its origins, anti-monarchical, and the Constituante had tried to establish a monarchical regime whereby executive and legislative powers could be shared with the king, the situation changed with the king's abortive escape from Paris to Varennes on the night of 20 June, 1791. Fears that the Revolution was in danger were exacerbated by support for the monarchy from Austria, birthplace of Queen Marie Antoinette. On 20 April, 1792, France declared war on Austria, as the Austrian emperor and the king of Prussia prepared a joint invasion, and marched on Paris, defeating revolutionary armies on their route, until they were turned back at the Battle of Valmy on 20 September, 1792.

The royal family was imprisoned following an attack on their home in the Tuileries Palace. Louis XVI was guillotined on 21 January, 1793. External threats were enjoined by a need for internal security; this led to further repression and to the Terror, especially under Robespierre. In the meantime the revolutionary armies continued to win battles abroad, occupying Belgium, the Rhineland, Savoy and Nice by April 1793.

In the spring of 1793 a coalition between Austria, Prussia and Great Britain led to further French defeats; then a year later the French defeated the Austrians at Fleurus and reoccupied Belgium (26 June, 1794). In the meantime Robespierre was overthrown on 27-28 July. 1794 (Thermidor). After his execution the Republicans would return to the liberal principles of the Declaration of the Rights of Man.

REVOLUTION IN FRANCE, 1789–93

- ▨ area of 'Great Fear' agrarian revolt
- ▮ major town in which a revolutionary committee replaced the town council, 1789
- ▮ major town in which a revolutionary committee shared power with the town council, 1789
- ▨ centre of counter revolution, 1792–93
- sustained Federalist resistance, 1793
- Federalist and other civil unrest, 1793
- → advance of French revolutionary armies
- → advance of European anti-revolutionary armies
- ✕ French victory
- ✕ European victory
- •••• naval blockade
- occupied by France, 1792–93

North Sea

NETHERLANDS

HOLY ROMAN EMPIRE

R. Rhine

Dunkirk

Sept. 1793 Hondschoote

Brussels

March 1793 Neerwinden

Cologne

Lille

Nov. 1793 Jemappes

Mons

June 1794 Fleurus

Coblenz

Arras

Amiens

Oct. 1793 Wattignies

AUSTRIAN NETHERLANDS

Mainz

Rouen

R. Seine

Caen

Reims

R. Meuse

Metz

Dec. 1793 Wissembourg

Landau

Paris

Sept. 1792 Valmy

Varennes

Nancy

Strasbourg

Rennes

Troyes

R. Marne

R. Saône

Angers

Tours

Dijon

Besançon

to Prussia

SWISS CONFEDERATION

Nantes

R. Loire

Bourges

Poitiers

R. Vienne

R. Allier

Clermont Ferrand

Lyon

Savoy

R. Isère

ATLANTIC OCEAN

Limoges

F R A N C E

Grenoble

KINGDOM OF SARDINIA

Bordeaux

R. Garonne

Rhône R.

R. Durance

Montauban

Venaissin

Avignon

Monaco

to Sardinia

Bayonne

Toulouse

Nîmes

Montpellier

Marseille

Toulon

REP. OF GENOA

R. Ebro

Perpignan

ANDORRA

SPAIN

Mediterranean Sea

N

0   60 km

0   60 miles

THE NAPOLEONIC EMPIRE

"Every French soldier carries in his cartridge-pouch the baton of a Marshall of France."
Napoleon

This painting by Ingres, presented to the citizens of Liège after a state visit, shows Napoleon Bonaparte, at age 34, as first consul in 1803, striking the pose that was to become almost his hallmark, although it was also a common artistic convention in portraits of the period.

By 1812, Napoleon reached the height of his power. France had expanded into Catalonia, the Low Countries, to the Rhine and acquired parts of Italy and the Illyrian provinces on the Adriatic. Buttressed by family members ruling lands such as Spain, Westphalia, Naples and other allied countries, this edifice dominated all Europe except Great Britain. The Code Napoleon, a mixture of Germanic customary law and Roman law, was introduced into a number of European countries, a form of "judicial imperialism". Belgium still retains the Code, which also became the model for the civil codes of Quebec province, Canada and many other parts of the world, including the state of Louisiana.

Despite the apparent stability and coherence of the empire, its foundations were seriously undermined by various flaws. First, French territorial aggrandizement was predicated upon the humiliation of other countries. The Treaty of Pressburg (December 1805), preceded by Austria's defeat at Austerlitz, forced Austria to cede her Italian possessions to France; Tyrol and the Vorarlberg went to Bavaria, with a financial penalty of forty million francs. After being defeated at Wagram (July 1980), Austria, again victimized by the Peace of Schönbrunn, was compelled to cede her Dalmatian territories directly to France; western Galicia was divided between Russia and the grand duchy of Warsaw; further lands were added to Illyria, Salzburg to Bavaria. Austria was looted of eighty five million francs in reparation payment, and the Princess Marie-Louise was constrained to marry Napoleon.

Second, the sanctions imposed on Austria were mirrored by the ill-treatment of Prussia. By the Treaty of Tilsit (July 1807) between France and Prussia, the latter lost half of her territories: those west of the Elbe were taken to form the new states of Berg and Westphalia. Also, Prussian Poland was seized to create the grand duchy of Warsaw. The large financial penalty and the reduction of the Prussian army to 42,000 men rubbed salt into the wounds.

The dual maltreatment of Austria and Prussia served to commence administrative and military reform in these countries while they waited for an appropriate time to rejoin the fray.

Third, the Continental System was designed by France to prevent Great Britain from trading with other European nations. Its various decrees (Berlin, 1806; Milan, 1807) generated a British blockade producing important economic and military results. In November 1807, Portugal's refusal to join the System resulted in a French incursion, initiating the Peninsula War. The eventual guerrilla warfare waged by Spanish patriots together with Wellington's campaigns seriously drained the French army's resources. The system excluded many imports from Europe and when Russia withdrew in 1810, Napoleon attacked the tsar in 1812.

The problems encountered by a war on two fronts in Spain and eastern Europe occasioned new allied declarations of war, with Austrians, Prussians, Russians and Swedes advancing across Europe and an invasion of France. The total exhaustion of the Napoleonic imperial system and military resulted in an enforced abdication in April 1814.

THE NAPOLEONIC EMPIRE, c. 1812

☐ ruled directly by Napoleon

☐ ruled by members of Napoleon's family

☐ dependent state

N

0   200 km
0   200 miles

Arctic Circle

Iceland

ATLANTIC
OCEAN

Faeroe Is.
to Denmark

Shetland Is.

North
Sea

Scotland
• Edinburgh

Ireland
• Dublin

UNITED KINGDOM
OF GREAT BRITAIN
AND IRELAND

Wales   England

London

Channel Is.

SWEDEN

Finland
1809 to Russia

Bergen

Christiana

Helsingfors
Revel

St. Petersburg
Novgorod

Åland Is.

Stockholm

Gotland

Smolensk

Vilna

Gothenburg

Riga

DENMARK-NORWAY
United until 1814

Copenhagen

Baltic Sea

to Sweden

REP. OF
DANZIG

Königsberg
East
Prussia

Bialystok
1807 to Russia

RUSSIAN
EMPIRE

Helgoland
1807–14 to Br.

Hamburg
Bremen

1807–10
to Fr.

Brandenburg

Amsterdam
1810 to Fr.

Antwerp

Hannover Berlin

WESTPHALIA

GR. DUCHY
OF WARSAW Warsaw

PRUSSIA

Brussels

Cologne

Erfurt

Bohemia
Prague

Silesia

Cracow

Galicia

Ternopol
1809 to Russia

1812 to Russia

Bessarabia

Frankfurt

CONFEDERATION
OF THE RHINE

• Paris

• Orléans
• Tours

FRANCE

Munich

AUSTRIAN
EMPIRE

Vienna
Styria

Buda
(Ofen) Pest

Moldavia

Lyon

Bern
HELVETIA

Geneva
1798–1814 to Fr.

Milan

Carinthia

Hungary

Transylvania

occupied by Russia

Bordeaux

Turin Venice
ITALY

Banat

Illyrian Provinces

Bucharest

Belgrade

Wallachia

Toulouse

Marseille

LUCCA
Tuscany Florence

Corsica

Papal
States

Adriatic Sea

OTTOMAN EMPIRE

MONTENEGRO

Bulgaria

• Sofia

Constantinople

Oporto

Catalona
1808–13 to Fr.

Barcelona

Rome

NAPLES

Naples

Macedonia

Aegean
Sea

Thessaly

Madrid

SPAIN

Balearic Is.

Minorca
1798–1802 to Br.

SARDINIA

Corfu
1807–14 to Fr.

Ionian Is.

occupied by Britain

Athens

Gibraltar
to Spain

Ceuta
to Spain

Oran

MOROCCO

Algiers

ALGERIA

Bona

Mediterranean   Sea

Tunis

TUNISIA

Palermo

SICILY

Malta
1798 to Fr.
1800 to Br.

Crete

111

THE CONGRESS OF VIENNA

"It will be the province of ministers abroad, to inculcate in all quarters the importance of union, to the preservation of peace for which the powers have for so long and so gloriously contended and to keep down as far as possible the spirit of local intrigue which has proved no less fatal to the repose of states than the personal ambitions of their sovereigns."
Viscount Catlereagh in a letter to the British ambassador to Vienna

With Louis XVIII restored to the French throne and Napoleon safely en route to Elba, peace was concluded between the Great Powers and France, with the signing of the First Treaty of Paris in May 1814. The congress was, therefore, an attempt by the Great Powers of Europe to make a constructive agreement for peace. Despite having been the enemy of the other European states, France was included in the Congress, because the other powers wanted to emphasize that normal relations between the French government and the rest of Europe had returned with the restoration of Louis XVIII. The idea was not to weaken Louis's position by humiliating France, which meant that France would be allowed to maintain the frontiers of 1792, although France would not recover her lost colonies. Nevertheless, France maintained Guadeloupe and most of her possessions in the West Indies and could maintain all her trading stations and commercial interests in India and fishing rights in the St. Lawrence and off Newfoundland. France had to reduce the size of her army, but was not required to disarm. France also had to surrender claims to territories conquered in Germany, Italy, Switzerland and the Low Countries.

The Congress of Vienna was held between September 1814 and June 1815, and continued throughout the Hundred Days (March–June 1815) that followed Napoleon's return to France. It was signed on 9 June, 1815.

Every state of Europe was represented, including the papacy, with the notable exception of the Ottoman empire. The decisions of the Congress were dominated by the Great Powers, whose chief representatives were Castlereagh and Wellington (Britain); Metternich and Gentz (Austria); Alexander I, Capo d'Istria, Nesselrode, and Stein (Russia); Hardenberg (Prussia); and Talleyrand (France).

The terms of the Second Treaty of Paris were harsher (20 November, 1815). France was offered her 1789 frontiers, and lost parts of Belgian territory and most of Savoy. France also had to return the art treasures that had been looted during the Napoleonic Wars and pay a war indemnity of 700 million francs and allow the allies to garrison her fortresses for five years.

The general principle of balance of power had been that the Great Powers should obtain the territory, or its equivalent, that each had held in 1805. Only Russia would obtain more by gaining a large part of Poland, including Warsaw, which British and Austrian opinion felt upset the balance of power.

Prussia gained Polish territory, half of Saxony and the Province of the Rhine. British interests concerned the creation of a central European bloc to provide security against French and Russian ambitions, leaving Austria as the dominant power in central Europe for the next fifty years and allowing Britain to relinquish her continental commitments. Austria gained Venetia and recovered Lombardy in Italy and became effective head of the German federation.

Holland and Belgium were united into one short-lived kingdom, under Dutch rule. Britain would retain Helgoland, Malta, Mauritius, Trinidad, St. Lucia, Tobago, the Cape of Good Hope and Ceylon, also gaining a protectorate over the Ionian Isles in the eastern Mediterranean.

The Congress of Vienna settled the peace of Europe for the next fifty years. It was a historical bridge between one period and another.

EUROPE AFTER THE TREATY OF VIENNA

━━━ German confederation

STATE UNIFICATION

In Germany and Italy, cultural unity provided a basis for political movements to unify a number of separate states into a larger whole. Existing small states Prussia and Piedmont-Sardinia were instrumental in achieving unification. Bismarck and Cavour were probably motivated more by the interests of their respective states than nationalism. Napoleon III favoured a powerful Prussia in northern Germany and promoted Piedmontese expansion to include Lombady-Venetia, Parma, Modena and Romagna within an Italian federation under papal presidency. This alliance, aimed at destroying Austrian power in Italy, triggered a war whereby the Franco-Piedmontese armies crushed the Austrians.

In June 1860, Garibaldi took a band of volunteers to Sicily. Historians debate his relationship with King Victor Emmanuel of Piedmont, who could have prevented the campaign. Garibaldi's success caused Cavour to invade the papal states, to prevent Garibaldi's invading Rome (garrisoned by France since 1848) to prevent French or Austrian intervention. The halting of Garibaldi at the Volturno was followed by plebiscites resulting in the union of Sicily, Naples, Umbria and the

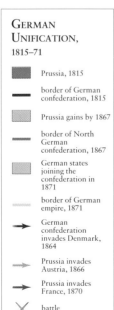

GERMAN UNIFICATION, 1815–71

- Prussia, 1815
- border of German confederation, 1815
- Prussia gains by 1867
- border of North German confederation, 1867
- German states joining the confederation in 1871
- border of German empire, 1871
- German confederation invades Denmark, 1864
- Prussia invades Austria, 1866
- Prussia invades France, 1870
- battle

Marches of Ancona with Piedmont, leading to the proclamation of a united Italy at Turin in 1861. In 1866, Italy acquired Venice following a Prussian alliance against Austria and after Prussia defeated France (1870), Italy entered and annexed Rome, confining the pope to Vatican City.

Prussian expansionism was based upon the policy of joining together her territorial blocs. In 1843, the German customs union was created, within which Prussia gained economic dominance. When Bismarck became chancellor (1862), a new realpolitik was introduced. In 1864, Austria and Prussia invaded Denmark over the Schleswig-Holstein Question and in 1865 took over the two duchies, with Prussia receiving Lauenburg. The victory preceded a war between Prussia and Austria in 1866 over Holstein and Prussian proposals reforming the German confederation. The defeat of Austria and her German allies allowed Prussia to annex most opposing states north of the River Main and to form the North German confederation. After Prussia defeated France (1870) and the annexation of Alsace-Lorraine, the south German states joined the confederation to create the German Reich (1874).

Count Camillo Benso di Cavour was an army officer before he turned to politics, serving as prime minister of Piedmont in 1852 until 1859 and again in 1860–1861. He secured foreign support for the idea of Italian unity.

1 Pontremoli, Tuscany, 1847 to Parma
2 Fivizzano, Tuscany, 1847 to Modena
3 Massa, 1829 to Modena
4 Duchy of Lucca, 1847 to Tuscany

UNIFICATION OF ITALY, 1859–1870

kingdom of Sardinia, 1815

annexed to kingdom of Sardinia, 1859

annexed to kingdom of Italy, 1860

annexed to kingdom of Italy, 1866

annexed to kingdom of Italy, 1870

→ route of Victor Emmanuel II, 1860

→ route of Garibaldi's Thousand, 1860

✗ battle

THE RUSSIAN REVOLUTION

"We will now proceed with the building of socialism." Vladimir Ilyich Lenin

The Russian revolutions of 1917 and their legacy have had a tremendous impact upon both European and world history, politics and belief systems in the twentieth century. It was not the successive military setbacks on the eastern front during the First World War that resulted directly in the February Revolution but rather the deteriorating economic conditions within Russia. In the meantime, inflation grew against a background of war profiteering, corruption and government instability. Yet, although the events of February 1917 were initially brought about by industrial unrest, it was the soldiers' refusal to fire on the crowds that turned the demonstrations into a revolt. Against a background of growing discontent, representatives of the Russian elite brought about the abdication of the tsar at Pskov on 15 March, 1917, in a failed attempt to stem the drift toward revolution. Meanwhile, the liberals of the Duma (Parliament) took temporary control of the country, establishing a provisional government under Prince Lvov, and later Alexander Kerensky; from the beginning this was weakened by sharing power with the Soviets.

In the eight months that followed, the provisional government introduced a number of reforms, but was hampered by its concern to continue the war with Germany. Furthermore, the provisional government was not a legitimately elected body and its position was weakened by its failure to establish a democratically elected Constituent Assembly. Ultimately it would be discredited by the failure of the Kerensky offensive in June, which provided yet another example of Russian strategies, being constantly subordinated to the war aims of her allies.

Although the Bolsheviks played no role in the February Revolution and suffered setbacks following the pre-emptive July coup; by the end of summer, their popularity was enhanced in the key urban centres by their role in the abortive Kornilov affair, and their demands for: "Peace, bread and land". Lenin returned to Russia on 10 October, as Kerensky, Prince Lvov's successor, faced growing opposition from the Petrograd Soviet.

In a climate of growing anarchy it became clear that the provisional government could neither continue the war nor finish it and in October 1917, Lenin and the Bolsheviks seized power in Petrograd with relatively little loss of life. The Bolsheviks arranged a cease-fire with the Germans, and in March 1918, peace proposals were negotiated between Russia and Germany at Brest-Litovsk.

The civil war that ensued was also a war of foreign intervention in which Russia's former allies, Britain, the United States and France, shifted their aims from containing the Germans on the eastern front to containing Bolshevism within Russia. The ravages of both the First World War and Civil War, in which between seventeen and eighteen million people lost their lives, were exacerbated by "War Communism", requisitioning and famine, which led to peasant disturbances and urban discontent in the winter of 1920–1921. The Bolsheviks crushed resistance, wiping out all opposition.

After Lenin's death on 21 January, 1921, opposition to Trotsky led to a struggle for the overall control of the party. Stalin, with the help of Kamenev and Zinoviev, rose to power.

Lenin returned from exile in Switzerland after the February revolution in 1917, leading the Bolshevik Revolution of the following November. He became the first leader of the new Soviet state, dying in office in 1924.

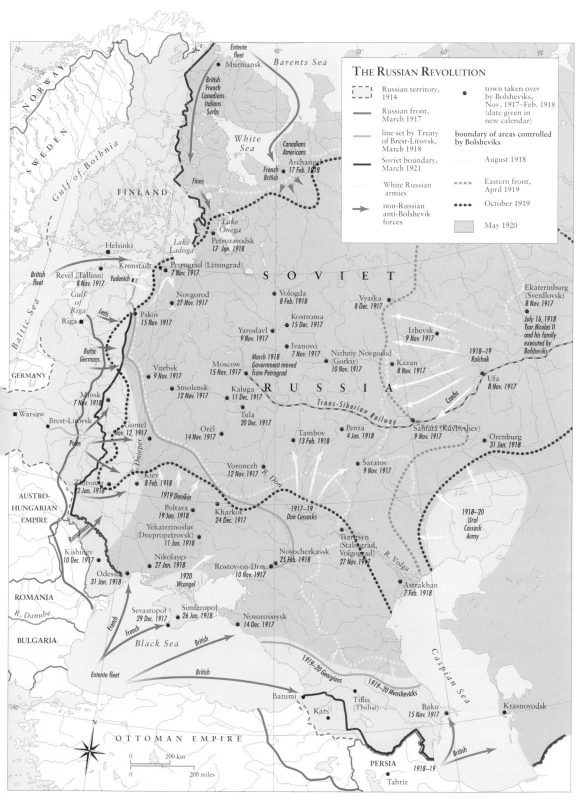

THE RUSSIAN REVOLUTION

- ⌐⌐⌐ Russian territory, 1914
- ● town taken over by Bolsheviks, Nov. 1917–Feb. 1918 (date given in new calendar)
- —— Russian front, March 1917
- —— line set by Treaty of Brest-Litovsk, March 1918
- —— Soviet boundary, March 1921
- —— White Russian armies
- → non-Russian anti-Bolshevik forces

boundary of areas controlled by Bolsheviks

- ········· August 1918
- ········· Eastern front, April 1919
- ●●●●●● October 1919
- ▓▓ May 1920

NORWAY

SWEDEN

Arctic Circle

Barents Sea

● Murmansk

British French Canadians Italians Serbs

White Sea

Canadians Americans

French British

Archangel 17 Feb. 1918

Gulf of Bothnia

Finns

FINLAND

Lake Onega

Petrozavodsk 17 Jan. 1918

Lake Ladoga

Helsinki

British fleet

Revel (Tallinn) 8 Nov. 1917

Kronstadt

Yudenich

Petrograd (Leningrad) 7 Nov. 1917

S O V I E T

Gulf of Riga

Riga

Letts

Pskov 15 Nov. 1917

Novgorod 27 Nov. 1917

Vologda 8 Feb. 1918

Vyatka 8 Dec. 1917

Ekaterinburg (Sverdlovsk) 8 Nov. 1917

July 16, 1918 Tsar Nicolas II and his family executed by Bolsheviks

Baltic Sea

Baltic Germans

Vitebsk 9 Nov. 1917

Kostroma 15 Dec. 1917

Izhevsk 9 Nov. 1917

Yaroslavl 9 Nov. 1917

1918–19 Kolchak

GERMANY

Ivanovo 7 Nov. 1917

Moscow 15 Nov. 1917

March 1918 Government moved from Petrograd

Nizhniy Novgorod (Gorkiy) 10 Nov. 1917

Kazan 8 Nov. 1917

Ufa 8 Nov. 1917

R U S S I A

Minsk 7 Nov. 1918

Smolensk 12 Nov. 1917

Kaluga 11 Dec. 1917

Czechs

Warsaw

Brest-Litovsk

Tula 20 Dec. 1917

Trans-Siberian Railway

Samara (Kuybyshev) 9 Nov. 1917

Gomel Nov. 12, 1917

Poles

Dnieper

Orël 14 Nov. 1917

Tambov 13 Feb. 1918

Penza 4 Jan. 1918

Orenburg 31 Jan. 1918

AUSTRO-HUNGARIAN EMPIRE

Zhitomir 2 Jan. 1918

Kiev 8 Feb. 1918

1919 Denikin

Voronezh 12 Nov. 1917

R. Don

Saratov 9 Nov. 1917

1918–20 Ural Cossack Army

Poltava 19 Jan. 1918

Kharkov 24 Dec. 1917

1917–19 Don Cossacks

Yekaterinoslav (Dnepropetrovsk) 11 Jan. 1918

Tsaritsyn (Stalingrad, Volgograd) 27 Nov. 1917

R. Volga

Kishinev 10 Dec. 1917

Romanians

Nikolayev 27 Jan. 1918

Novocherkassk 25 Feb. 1918

Rostov-on-Don 10 Nov. 1917

Odessa 31 Jan. 1918

1920 Wrangel

Astrakhan 7 Feb. 1918

ROMANIA

R. Danube

BULGARIA

French

Sevastopol 29 Dec. 1917

Simferopol 26 Jan. 1918

Novorossiysk 14 Dec. 1917

French

Black Sea

British

British

Entente fleet

British

Caspian Sea

Krasnovodsk

1919–20 Georgians

1919–20 Mensheviks

OTTOMAN EMPIRE

Batumi

Kars

Tiflis (Tbilisi)

Baku 15 Nov. 1917

British

N

0   200 km

0   200 miles

PERSIA

1918–19

Tabriz

Entente fleet

THE NEW RUSSIA

"The arrests
mounted into
the millions; the
testimony of the
survivors is
unanimous
regarding
crowded prison
cells and teem-
ing forced
labour camps.
Most of the
prisoners were
utterly bewil-
dered by the fate
which had
befallen them."
Merle Fainsod

By the end of the 1930s, the Soviet Union had been through a tremendous upheaval. Between seventeen and eighteen million people had been lost in the First World War and the Civil War and a large number through famine and disease. A repressive totalitarian system had been put in place to maintain in power a monolithic party that had no legitimate democratic authority.

After the death of Lenin, Stalin, once in power, secured his position through ruthless policies of industrialization, collectivization and a system of terror and repression that grew with the spread of the Gulag system of "corrective labour" — linked with the Great Purges, or Yezhovschine, of 1936–1941, named after the eponymous Commisar for Internal Affairs from September 1936 to July 1938, Nicholas Yezhov, during which it has been estimated that ten million were arrested and three million executed.

Despite this the vision of a new Russia that was a thriving and happy society was carefully fostered by the Soviet government and its organs. They harnessed the forces of Socialist Realist art and cinema, to provide images of happy agricultural workers and tractor drivers, gathering the harvests, alongside loyal Stakhanovites (named after Alexis Stakhanov, a coal miner who persistently exceeded his allotted quota), toiling cheerfully in the mines and factories, doubling or tripling production levels and yields.

In industry priority was given to producers' goods over consumer goods, and all available resources were channelled into heavy industry. Before the Great Patriotic War, the Stalinist organization of the Soviet economy was realized through a series of three Five-Year Plans involving the expansion of industry. Although production rates were generally increased, this was often at the expense of quality. Despite the hardships in which workers accused of industrial sabotage were sent to the Gulag, on the outbreak of war, the foundations of an industrial base had been well laid.

Collectivization was forced upon the countryside and would change the lives of over 75 per cent of the Soviet population. By 1937, almost all cultivated land was in collective farms *(kolkhozi)* or state farms *(sovkhozi)* which were more directly controlled on factory lines by the state. In the Soviet Union many collective farms were inefficient.

With the increase in international tensions in the 1930s, an even more ferocious event was about to be unleashed on the Soviet people. On the eve of the German invasion in 1941, agricultural production still had not returned to its 1928 levels.

A poster designed by Victor Deni, Enemies of the Five-Year-Plan, *1928–1933.*

THE NEW RUSSIA

— international border

— Soviet Socialist Republic
(SSR) border

- - - Autonomous Soviet Socialist
Republic (ASSR) border

— Transcaucasian Soviet
Federative Socialist Republic
(SFSR) border, 1922–36

● city experiencing
major population
growth, 1926–39

△ engineering/
armament industry

coal mining

iron ore mining

▲ oil extraction

area of major famine

famine conditions
widespread

● port used by American
Relief Administration

route of foreign-supplied
relief

— other major rail route

Barents Sea

Arctic Circle

White Sea

Karelian ASSR 1924

Komi ASSR 1936

R. Ob'

Archangel

FINLAND

Lake Onega

Lake Ladoga

Gulf of Bothnia

Hango

Helsinki

Tallinn

Leningrad

ESTONIA

Russian Socialist Federative Socialist Republic 1917

Gulf of Riga

LATVIA Riga

LITHUANIA

Yaroslavl

Ivanovo

Mori ASSR 1936

GERMANY E.Prussia

Baltic Sea

Chuvash ASSR 1934

Kazan

Tatar ASSR

Baskir ASSR

Warsaw

White Russia SSR 1919

Moscow

Mordvinian ASSR 1934

Samara (Kuybyshev)

POLAND

R. Dnieper

CZE.

Kiev

Ukraine 1917

Kharkov

Voronezh

Saratov

R. Don

Kazakh ASSR 1932

ROMANIA

Krivoy Rog

Yekaterinoslav (Dnepropetrovsk)

Donetsk

Zaporozhye

Rostov-on-Don

Tsaritsyn (Stalingrad, Volgograd)

R. Volga

Kalmyk ASSR 1936

Odessa

R. Danube

BULGARIA

Black Sea

Sevastopol

Novorossiisk

N. Ossetian ASSR 1936

Kabardo-Balkar ASSR 1936

Daghestan ASSR 1932

Caspian Sea

Chechen-Ingush ASSR 1936

Batumi

Georgian ASSR 1936

Tiflis (Tbilisi)

Azerbaijan ASSR 1936

Krasnovodsk

Baku

Armenian ASSR 1936

TURKEY

0   200 km

0   200 miles

N

PART VII: IMPERIAL ECHOES

The First World War ended a century of scientific, industrial and cultural progress. Events conspired against Europe: war, nationalism, imperialism, the alliance systems, armed peace and a total failure to establish a system of international arbitration that ensured carnage on the battlefield and the spread of a European into a global war. This conflict gave a new impetus to nationalisms that were developing in Asia and Africa even before 1914. Anti-imperial feeling and failure to repress it demonstrated structural weaknesses in Europe, and the nationalisms of colonial peoples continued until they achieved independence after the Second World War.

The breakdown of the balance of power in 1914, the impact of war, chaos, poverty and hunger in east and central Europe, and badly designed peace treaties left a legacy of hatred and revenge that raged after 1945. The war also brought into focus the economic decline of Europe compared with the United States, and the U.S.-exported 1929 stock market crash and the following Depression exacerbated problems caused by debts and war reparation payments. The next war threw into sharp relief Europe's exhaustion and imperial overstretch, a humiliating counterpoint to apparent strength and pride at the end of the New Imperialist surge in the late nineteenth century.

The decades before World War I saw a relative decline in religious idealism and an increase in secular attacks on religion as demonstrated by Bismarck's Kulturkampf, the French Third Republic's onslaught on the Roman Catholic Church after the Boulanger Crisis and the hostility between the new Italian state and the pope. British urbanization and the failure of the Anglican Church to build enough places of worship in towns allowed congregations to drift away, with many working class men and women switching to dissenting movements such as Methodism. The spread of education and literacy allowed the general population to be more aware of foreign affairs. The breakdown in rural extended kinship patterns and community in the face of industrialization produced a new hierarchy of values whereby nationalism exalted the motherland and fatherland on whose altars the good patriot should sacrifice himself. This new sense of identity was subject to manipulation by governments and newspapers raising the spectre of chauvinism, fanaticism and hysteria in times of national crisis. The breakdown in the old Concert of Europe meant the lack of an arbitration system to orchestrate diplomatic peace processes. The result was mistrust leading to even more secret diplomacy and foreign policies. Even when governments desired moderation, the newly literate populace sometimes imagined insults to national pride, thereby exerting undue pressures on government. New ideologies and movements were spawned: Russian state-sponsored Pan-Slavism; the Pan-German Alldeutscher Verband; French revanchists uniting behind General Boulanger, advocating war to regain Alsace-Lorraine; the Action Française with Charles Maurras's ideal of total nationalism; extremist Italian irredentism; and British imperialism, jingoism and the Primrose League. Exaggerated national egos fuelled an aggressive realpolitik, first introduced in a moderate form by Bismarck. Reasons of state became the ideal and could legitimize any policy.

Europe rapidly deteriorated into an armed peace with two opposing camps competing in military and naval arms races: the Triple Alliance and the Triple Entente. Both systems were permanently renewing themselves as long as the other existed. Now any crisis, however minor, could escalate out of all proportion and blow up as one did in 1914. Serious crises were endemic: the first Moroccan Crisis between France and Germany (1905); the Bosnia-Herzegovina Crisis between Russia and Austria-Hungary (1908); the second Moroccan Crisis between the same protagonists (1911); the crises surrounding the Balkan Wars involving Russia and Austria-Hungary (1913); and finally, the Black Hand's murder of Archduke Franz Ferdinand in Sarajevo in 1914, which tipped Europe into disaster.

European statesmen considered that the scramble for empire would be a safety valve. The emergence of new states in Europe — Italy and Germany — reduced opportunities for expansion in Europe. The virtual end of free trade and the establishment of protectionism by industrializing countries generated a search for new overseas markets and their seizure by all force necessary. The development of new technologies aided imperialism: steamships needed regular coaling stations like Aden and Mauritius, stepping-stones to British India and French Indochina respectively; and the innovation of ships with refrigeration compartments meant food could be transported longer distances to feed the industrial, urbanized masses. The rifle and the machine-gun made violent policies easier but not without the occasional mishap, such as Zulus slaughtering a British force at Isandhlwana and the Ethiopians overwhelming an Italian force at Adowa. The French became very careful when Dahomey's fighting women leaped from jungle cover wielding spears. Nevertheless, the colonization of the world rolled on and Europeans transported the balance of power to Africa and Asia. Jules Ferry, French premier in 1881 and supporter of imperialist mercantilism, saw the conquest of Tunisia as being restitution for the loss of Alsace-Lorraine. All imperial powers sought to partition areas, seek compensation and create buffer states. Siam, Iran and Afghanistan retained independence to separate France and Britain, or Britain and Russia.

Equality of commercial access was also important, as evidenced in 1900, when Europeans endorsed the United States suggestion of an Open Door policy in China and in 1906 when a conference at Algeciras announced such equality regarding Morocco. By 1914, all continents were held in thrall, except where the Monroe Doctrine held sway and the great powers seemed to have settled their colonial differences bilaterally.

Even while pursuing the New Imperialism, the European states faced almost constant rebellion. Both Africa and Asia provide examples of determined stands by peoples seeking independence, resisting encroachment and establishing nationalist parties and associations. In Indochina, De Tham fought the French until 1913, the year that saw the foundation of Vietnam Quang Phuc Ho (Association for the Restoration of Vietnam), a revolutionary organization started by Phan Boi Chau. In Africa, Britain met fierce resistance from the

Ashanti, Zulu and Matabele, while tyrannical German rule provoked a Herero revolt in South-West Africa (1904) after many had been subject to genocide; the anti-German Maji-Maji Rebellion (1905) in Tanganyika is another example. Some anti-colonialist movements were traditionalist and religious, notably the Mahdi's seizure of the Sudan in 1881. A holy war against the Dutch in northern Sumatra (1881–1908), the Chinese Boxer uprising (1900) and the attack on foreign legations in Peking brought fearful European retaliation. More peaceful means were explored by the Indian National Congress founded in 1885, the Egyptian National Party (1899) and Egyptian People's Party (1907). The year 1912 saw the birth of the Indonesian National Party (Sarekat Islam) and the South African National Congress. The First World War gave new encouragement to Asian and African nationalisms. In China, Sun Yat-sen saw the Japanese victory over Russia in 1904–1905 as the "defeat of the West by the East", showing the art of the possible. In 1916, major anti-Russian uprisings took place in Muslim central Asia; the Saharan Senussi helped an anti-French rebellion in Tunisia (1915–1916), while France also had to cope with rebellion in Annam (1916); and the British had to suppress an anti-settler movement in Nyasaland. Although these and other nationalist activities stimulated resistance of those resentful and in despair, little was achieved except that European rule was exposed as insecure and myths grew that in later years led to the collapse of European imperialism and freedom for dominated peoples. The colonial powers faced further difficulties after 1918, especially with the inheritance of League of Nations' mandates in the Middle East. In Syria, the French suppressed a nationwide revolt (1925–1927). Between 1935 and 1939, Britain faced a large Arab revolt in opposition to Jewish immigration into Palestine, having granted independence to Egypt (1922) while retaining control of the Suez Canal and military matters. Elsewhere in North Africa, the 1930s saw early nationalist movements applying pressure on the French in Morocco, Algeria and Tunisia. In Asia, Gandhi linked nationalism to Hinduism and engaged in civil disobedience campaigns against British India, thereby raising the profile of the Indian National Congress. Eventually the British were persuaded to introduce the Government of India Act (1935), which allowed political participation in central and provincial governments. By 1937, the Congress controlled a majority of the provincial ones.

The depression and subsequent unemployment were a major factor in causing unrest. The West Indies saw strikes and riots, as did the Gold Coast, which again pressured the British into rethinking colonial policy. Ceylon was given a new constitution in 1931 and Burma was split from India and given a degree of autonomy in 1935. Other colonial powers adopted a recalcitrant attitude of no concession. French Indochina experienced outbreaks of violence, leading to the creation of the Vietminh by Ho Chi Minh in 1941. The Dutch East Indies saw unsuccessful Communist outbreaks demanding self-determination. Eventually, the Second World War changed the nature of European colonialism in Asia. The failure of the imperial powers in the face of Japanese aggression gave an impetus to popular nationalisms and after 1945, the Europeans either granted independence or were kicked out.

The colonial experience demonstrated the inherent fragility of European power. The Great War of 1914–1918 ruined Europe financially and wiped out so much youth that some European towns and villages were denuded of an entire generation of young men. The advent of the United States into the war (April 1917) turned the tide for the Entente powers but introduced President Wilson into European politics. His peace aims were idealistic and predicated upon ignorance of Europe and his plans for the post-war world ushered in a new diplomacy based upon a League of Nations that the U.S. senate so disliked that the United States was prevented from joining. However, his failure and that of all statesmen at Versailles to address the nationality issue in its entirety left a legacy of hatred, especially after the victors penalized the defeated with territorial losses and reparations, and saddled the Germans with a war-guilt clause. According to A. J. P. Taylor, a controversial British historian, the Second World War was fought to rewrite Versailles. For Europe, the inter-war years were characterized by moral regression and political insanity in an apparent lemming-like drive to shrug off the last vestiges of culture and civilization. The new Europe of Versailles and its associated treaties destroyed Austria-Hungary and constructed a jigsaw of small successor states, none being economically viable and all containing ethnic minorities. The dissolution of the Habsburg empire removed the last foreign policy restraint from Germany, a factor that Hitler rapidly noted and appreciated.

The fragmentation of Europe was extensive and posed infinite dilemmas for the future. The new states were generally aggrieved at not receiving enough territory or resentful that kinfolk were minorities in other countries. The new states included Czechoslovakia, a re-established Poland, Finland, Estonia, Latvia and Lithuania, while others were enlarged, such as Romania and the hotchpotch state of Yugoslavia. This was based upon an expanded Serbia, ushering in a political nightmare whose inhabitants are still trying to eradicate each other, giving humanity an exercise in ethnic cleansing. The nadir of inter-war Europe appeared in its mix of ethnic grievances, compounded by the economic poverty and decline during the Great Depression.

The farrago of small, strategically vulnerable states faced two new economic, social and ideological systems challenging and criticizing capitalism and democracy. In Italy, Mussolini coined the term "totalitarianism" when building the Fascist Party, while the Soviet Union offered the world a Communist blueprint. More significant was the German appointment of Adolf Hitler as chancellor, then führer. Europe was drawing the lines for renewed conflict. Fascist and military dictatorships spread rapidly, while the League of Nations collapsed in the face of the Spanish Civil War, Italy's attack on Abyssinia and the Japanese invasion of Manchuria. European democracies were outnumbered and still recovering from the Depression, now faced darkness in six years of organized savagery.

GLOBAL EMPIRES

EUROPEAN EXPLORATION AND COLONIZATION

→ Norwegians, Icelanders, c. 1000

→ Friar Rubruck, 1253–55

→ Nicolo and Maffeo Polo, 1262

→ Marco Polo, 1272–95

Portugese discover Madeira c. 1419, Azores c. 1427

→ King Manuel of Portugal sends expedition west to locate Antillia, unsuccessful

→ Bristol Merchants attempt to find "Isles of Brazil", 1480–81

→ Bartholomew Diaz, 1496–88

→ Christopher Columbus, 1492–93 (1st voyage)

→ John Cabot, 1497 (1st voyage)

→ Amerigo Vespucci, 1499 (2nd voyage)

→ Vasco de Gama, 1427–98

→ Amerigo Vespucci, 1501

→ Magellan (del Cano after Magellan's death), 1521–22

→ Drake, 1577–80

→ Abel Tasman, 1642–43

main directions of European colonization or control, 1450–1600

→ Spanish

→ Portuguese

→ English

→ French

→ Dutch

→ Russian

▨ under European colonization or control mid. 17th C.

As a symbol of domination, Queen Victoria looks across yet another possession, this time Cape Town, South Africa.

From the late 1400s Europeans began to sail the oceans, trading, conquering and colonizing the world. In this painting by Diego
Velasquez, Christopher Columbus (Cristobal Colon), navigator and
explorer who made four voyages across the Atlantic, offers the New
World to the Catholic king of Spain.

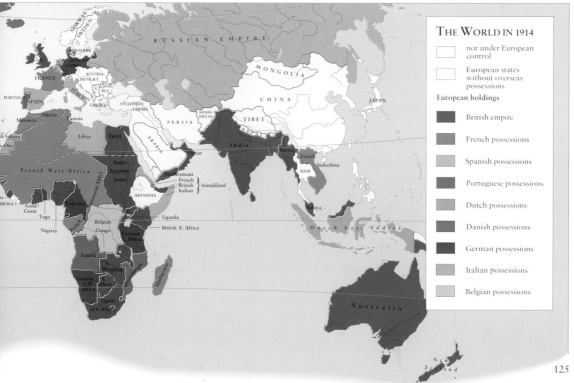

THE WORLD IN 1914

- not under European control
- European states without overseas possessions

European holdings

- British empire
- French possessions
- Spanish possessions
- Portuguese possessions
- Dutch possessions
- Danish possessions
- German possessions
- Italian possessions
- Belgian possessions

"The colonies
are millstones
round our
neck."
Disraeli, 1852

The late nineteenth century introduced the "New Imperialism", a period when the great powers partitioned the world into economic and political empires. Historical explanations for this phenomenon are legion, such as the Marxist surplus capital theory, export of excess population, strategic defence of existing empire and the belief that empire aided the balance of power and a nation's international prestige.

Prior to 1871, European overseas possessions were confined to British India and South Africa, the Dutch East Indies, French Algeria and Cochin-China, Spanish Cuba and Philippines and Russian Siberia and central Asia. Otherwise, European influence was limited to trading stations (Lagos, Hong Kong), Chinese treaty ports such as Shanghai and strategic posts (Aden). The new expansionism is best exemplified by the "scramble of Africa". The French empire spread throughout north and west Africa and Madagascar; the Germans moved into German East Africa, South-West Africa, the Cameroons and Togoland; Britain acquired Egypt, the Sudan, Kenya, Uganda, the Rhodesias, Nyasaland, Nigeria and the Gold Coast; Leopold II of Belgium gained the Congo as a personal possession; the Portuguese expanded their trading stations into Angola and Mozambique; and the Italians seized Eritrea, parts of Somaliland and Libya but failed to capture Abyssinia, the Italian army being overwhelmed at Adowa (1896). China provided the other main area of competition in the "battle for concessions" when interested powers jockeyed for commercial advantages, development projects and territory. Although various ports were lost to European powers and areas penetrated economically (most noticeably Britain controlling the River Yangtze-Kiang Basin trade), China managed to retain independence. Even the Sino-Japanese War (1895) and the loss of Formosa failed to destroy the remnants of Chinese sovereignty. Events adjacent to China illustrate the peculiar British approach to empire. Despite Disraeli's declaration that colonies were a drain on economic resources, Britain continued to acquire lands to safeguard influence and to act as a bulwark for existing empire. Hence, when France added Tonking (1885) and Laos (1893) to Cambodia and Cochin-China, Britain acquired Burma (1886) and the two powers divided Siam into spheres of influence. Elsewhere in the Pacific, Britain took Fiji, parts of Borneo and New Guinea; other islands were the subject of British, French and German competition. By 1914, Britain had accumulated 20 per cent of the world's land surface, one-quarter of the world's population, and all the trade routes in the Indian Ocean. Simultaneously, non-European empires threatened European dominance; the Spanish-American War (1898) allowed the United States to obtain Cuba, Puerto Rico, Guam and the Philippines; Hawaii was annexed the same year, but Cuba was granted independence in 1902, although remaining under U.S. influence. Nationalism and imperialism propelled Japan into wars against China (1895) and Russia (1905), gaining Formosa (1895), the lease of the Liaotung Peninsula, south Sakhalin and considerable rights in south Manchuria and recognition of Japanese supremacy in Korea, formally annexed in 1910.

The First World War provided nationalists with an opportunity to voice their resentment against imperial control. When Britain made Egypt a protectorate (1914), latent anti-British feelings sprang forth. French possessions were also susceptible to uprisings in Tunisia (1915–1916), while Italy had never crushed the Sanusi tribesmen in Libya. The peace treaties ending World War I altered the imperial map: in the Middle East, Britain was given Palestine, Transjordan and Iraq, and France gained Lebanon and Syria, all as League of Nations mandates. Germany's former African possessions were mandated to Britain (Tanganyika) and South Africa (South-West Africa), while Britain and France shared Togoland and the Cameroons. In the Far East, Japan and Australia divided Germany's Pacific islands. The inter-war years exposed the weaknesses of the imperial powers: rule was gradually understood to be temporary as expressed in the new concept of British "dominion" and in the mandate system itself. Nationalist movements grew as a result of armed conflict such as that led by Abdel-Krim against France and Spain (1921–1926). Educated elites commenced mobilization of wider support as in Gandhi's Indian civil disobedience campaign. Elsewhere, in Asia, Communist revolts (1926) burst out in the Dutch East Indies and such militancy exemplified a group of emerging radical leaders such as Ho Chi Minh in Vietnam, Nehru in India and Sukarno in Indonesia. The Second World War further explored the frailty of empire with the loss of colonies to Japan and the sheer exhaustion of the imperialists shown in financial, military and demographic terms.

Reaction against imperialism articulated itself in a number of ways: indigenous nationalism, especially in Algeria and Southeast Asia; pressure exerted by the United States desiring emancipation and new markets, and the USSR's offering ideological blueprints based on class struggle and revolution; and worldwide anti-colonization being given a forum in the United Nations, allowing the non-aligned a stage, resulting in the uncompromising 1960 Declaration on the Granting of Independence to Colonial Countries and Peoples.

The speed of de-colonization was probably occasioned by military weakness, and new plans for European cooperation and economic integration made Europe less expansionist with a realization that it had shrunk in terms of power and influence. France was pushed out of southeast Asia by Ho Chi Minh (1954) and Algeria became independent in 1962. Most French colonies were freed in 1960, many joining a French community. Spain liberated most of its African colonies peacefully, but Nehru seized Portugal's Indian colonies while guerrilla liberation movements brought independence to Angola and Mozambique (1974). The Dutch faced similar problems, unable to reassert authority in the East Indies. The UN arranged a transfer of sovereignty in 1949; next it helped the Belgian Congo after 1960. Britain, pressured into emancipating the Indian empire (1947), conferred independence in Africa from 1957 onwards. After the 1950s, some remnants of colonialism remained, such as Rhodesia.

THE ROAD TO SELF-DESTRUCTION

INVESTMENTS IN ARMS, 1880, 1914

1880
1914

investment in millions of pounds

140
120
100
80
60
40
20
0

Germany
Austro-Hungary
Italy
Great Britain
Russia
France

"Fritz," the giant steam hammer at a Krupps armament works, c. 1914.

The creation of the German Reich (1871) ushered in a new balance of power. All states accepted the change except France, which lost Alsace-Lorraine and felt increasingly isolated over colonial differences with Britain and Italy. When Bismarck fell from power (1890), his foreign policy of alleviating international tension ended. Imperial antagonism, the non-renewal of the Reinsurance Treaty with Russia, and the character of Kaiser Wilhelm all combined to aggravate the international system. All major states sought security but were prepared to seek varied combinations of alliance partners to achieve their aims. Russia attempted to prevent any unfriendly power from controlling the Straits at Constantinople and feared Austro-Hungarian influence spreading into the Balkans and to this end signed military conventions with Bulgaria (1902) and Serbia (1903). Britain wanted to protect her empire and sought ways of preventing perceived Russian expansion in Persia and Afghanistan as a thrust toward India. A 1907 Anglo-Russian agreement allayed fears and prepared the way for the Triple Entente. France drew closer to Russia when the failure of the Reinsurance Treaty forced Russia to find a new partner. The need to industrialize required financial loans, and the closure of the Berlin stock exchange to such transactions prevented Russia's borrowing to rearm and build. Stategic railways had opened the way to a Franco-Russian alliance in 1894. The Anglo-French Entente (1904) enabled the two countries to settle their differences over Morocco and Egypt. The entente faced its first test in the 1905–1906 Morocco Crisis; the Anglo-French-Russian Triple Entente followed in 1907. A naval arms race between Germany and Britain in battleship construction increased tensions brought to a head in the second Moroccan Crisis, when France occupied Fez. The dispatch of a German warship and the resultant crisis were only resolved by an agreement over a French protectorate in Morocco, with German compensation in the Cameroons. The fluid situation allowed Italy to seize Tripoli and the Dodecanese. The Balkans provided the other flash point. In 1908, Austria-Hungary annexed Bosnia-Herzegovina from the Turks, angering Serbia by destroying one element of its plans for a Greater Serbia. German support for the seizure intensified international problems and Russia saw a Germanic march on the Straits (Dardanelles). In 1909, Russia and Italy signed a secret Treaty of Racconigi to keep a Balkan status quo. The crisis also sealed the 1879 Austro-German alliance, tying the latter to Austrian aims in the Balkans. Further concern was caused by the Austro-Serb "Pig Wars" (1906–1911), unrest in Albania, and the two Balkan Wars of 1912 and 1913, which saw Turkey virtually thrown out of Europe, and large territories added to Greece, Bulgaria and Serbia, the last being disappointed over the non-acquisition of an Adriatic outlet due to Austrian interference. By 1914, German Weltpolitik challenged the old imperial powers, and Germany and Austria felt encircled by the Entente. When Archduke Franz Ferdinand was killed in Sarajevo, Serbia appeared to reopen its ambitions, and the subsequent Austrian ultimatum backed by Germany was the final step to war and self-destruction.

Alliances on the Eve of War, July 1914

- Austro-German Alliance, 1879–1918
- Triple Alliance, 1882–1915
- Franco-Russian Alliance, 1894–1917
- Triple Entente, 1907–1917
- varying independence and nationalist movements sponsored by Russia, 1879–1914
- sympathetic to 'Central Powers'
- sympathetic to 'Entente Powers'
- neutrality guaranteed by United Kingdom
- neutral

WORLD WAR I

The First World War inaugurated new modes of warfare, resulting in hitherto unknown destruction of human life, material and landscape. When war began in August 1914, all countries based their plans on a short war, but best-laid plans went astray; the conflict developed into long lines of entrenched armies in almost immovable siege-like conditions in a war of attrition. The German Schlieffen Plan intended to encircle and destroy the French Army by a sweeping hook through neutral Belgium, but nervousness in execution and events on Germany's eastern front drew troops from the west, allowing the Allies to consolidate their front into a 400-mile complex

WORLD WAR I

- Central powers
- Allied powers
- joining Allied powers at a later date
- declaration of war surrender
- Central powers attack, 1914
- Allied attack, 1914
- front line, late 1914
- Central powers attack, 1915–17
- Allied attack, 1915–17
- front line, mid 1917
- Central Powers occupation of Russia, Feb.–May 1918 and occupation of Georgia by Ottoman empire, May 1918
- Allied attack, 1918
- front line, Nov. 1918
- naval battle

of trenches and barbed wire extending from the English Channel to the Swiss frontier. The stalemate in the west occasioned total war, with intense mobilization of both people and industry. Various innovations attempted to end the deadlock; the Germans used poisoned gas at Ypres (April 1915) and the British the newly developed tank on the Somme (July 1916) and at Cambrai (November 1917). The land battle spread to the skies and seas in a hopeless search for victory. Primitive aircraft grew into sophisticated forms such as the Sopwith Camel and Fokker Triplane, and Germany developed the Zeppelin airship and Gotha long-range bomber capable of bombing enemy cities. Meanwhile, the Allies' naval blockade tried to starve the Central powers, stimulating a submarine counter-offensive. Continued stalemate led the Allies into opening new war fronts in Europe: landing in the Dardanelles (April 1915–January 1916) this staggered to a halt with over 200,000 casualties; likewise an attempt to help Serbia through Salonika, bogged down. The Italian entrance into the war on the Allied side in an attack on Austria on the Isonzo also failed.

On the eastern front, the Germans defeated a Russian invasion at Tannenberg (August 1914), while the Russians defeated Austria at Lemberg (September 1914). Despite a German offensive at Gorlice-Tarnow in 1915 and the Russian Brusilov advance in 1916, no decision resulted. Only when Russia dissolved into revolution did the Germans finally manage to advance through the Ukraine and force the Bolsheviks to sign the Treaty of Brest-Litovsk (December 1917). The entry of the United States into the conflict (6 April, 1917) after Germany declared unrestricted submarine warfare turned the tide for the Allies. The extra Allied manpower limited German territorial acquisitions in new offensives, the counter-attacks under Marshall Foch pushed back the Germans and the tank onslaught at Amiens (August 1918) was partially responsible for the German retreat to the Hindenburg Line. Austria's last offensive at the Piave against Italy (June 1918) failed and the Allies finally broke through enemy lines in Macedonia (September 1918); in the face of this advance the Bulgarian army collapsed. As a result of this deteriorating situation, General Ludendorff called for an armistice, thereby acknowledging the defeat of the Central powers. The mutiny of the German fleet (1918), revolutionary eruptions throughout Germany and the kaiser's abdication with the proclamation of a republic led to an armistice (11 November, 1918), ending a European conflagration that had spread to the Middle East, Africa and Asia. The victors now had to make the peace based upon U.S. president Wilson's Fourteen Points.

> "And by his smile, I knew that sullen hall. By his dead smile I knew we stood in Hell."
> *Wilfred Owen*

This detail of a painting by the British artist Paul Nash shows the Menin Road, giving an idea of the destruction and squalid horror of life on the western front between 1914 and 1918.

VERSAILLES, 1919

At the end of World War I, the Allies imposed a series of peace treaties upon the defeated Central Powers. From a European perspective the most important were Versailles on Germany, Trianon on Hungary and St. Germain on Austria.

Opening in January 1919, the Versailles conference sought to follow the Congress of Vienna (1814) in the redrawing the map of Europe. Taking certain principles into consideration, nationalist demands for independence in eastern and central Europe would receive attention using principles of democracy, freedom, self-determination and U.S. President Wilson's Fourteen Points.

The participants at Versailles sought to rationalize the incoherent mess that was the aftermath of war. Eventually, the three main political figures, Wilson, Lloyd George and Clemenceau, fought it out for their separate interests. Wilson wanted open diplomacy and a League of Nations. Lloyd George saw Britain as a naval and imperial power, viewing Germany as a bastion against France and Bolshevik Russia, and he also desired Germany's African colonies. Clemenceau sought revenge, a weakened Germany and four Allied military-controlled Rhine bridgeheads, eventually established by treaty.

Conflicting interests meant that Wilson's idealism remained unfulfilled. Ultimately, Germany lost territory to Poland, France, Belgium and Denmark; and was virtually disarmed. Germany also had its colonies seized as League of Nations mandates, had the Saarland occupied by French troops, and was saddled with a war guilt clause and huge reparations.

Austria-Hungary was sundered, leaving the rump states of Austria and Hungary.

The end product of these treaties were excessive German reparations, while a variety of peoples were still intermingled in new multinational states throughout central Europe and the Balkans. Throughout the region, railway communications and banking systems were fragmented, and economically viable areas were destroyed.

EUROPE IN 1914

EUROPE IN 1919

200 km

200 miles

N

Arctic Circle

Iceland
to Denmark

Norwegian
Sea

Faeroe Islands
to Denmark

N O R W A Y

S W E D E N

F I N L A N D

Helsinki
Tallinn
Leningrad

Oslo

Stockholm

ESTONIA

North
Sea

Riga

Baltic Sea

LATVIA

Glasgow
Edinburgh

DENMARK
Copenhagen

LITHUANIA
Kaunas

Königsberg

U.S.S.R.

UNITED KINGDOM

Liverpool

Hamburg

Danzig
free city under
League of Nations

East
Prussia

Birmingham
Amsterdam

Berlin

Warsaw

Brest Litovsk

Bristol

NETHERLANDS

London

Calais

Brussels

GERMANY

P O L A N D

BELGIUM

R. Rhine

Frankfurt

Prague

Cracow

Lvov

ATLANTIC
OCEAN

Paris

SAAR
autonomous under
League of Nations

CZECHOSLOVAKIA

Orleans

Vienna

F R A N C E

Bern
SWITZ.

AUSTRIA HUNGARY

Budapest

R O M A N I A

Lyon

Trieste

Bucharest

Bordeaux

Milan

Belgrade

R. Danube

Black Sea

Genoa

Venice

YUGOSLAVIA

BULGARIA

Marseille

ANDORRA

Adriatic Sea

Sofia

TURKEY

PORTUGAL

Barcelona

I T A L Y

Rome

ALBANIA

Aegean
Sea

Lisbon

Madrid

S P A I N

Naples

GREECE

Smyrna

Balearic Is.

Athens

Alicante

Italian
occupied

Cádiz

Gibraltar
to Great Britain
international
zone

Almeria

M e d i t e r r a n e a n

Tangier

Morocco
to France

A l g e r i a
to France

Tunisia
to France

S e a

Libya
to Italy

THE GREAT DEPRESSION

All over Europe workers were laid off in huge numbers. In towns like Jarrow in the northeast of England, the only people working were the few organizing the soup kitchens for the relief of the unemployed.

The Great Depression began in 1929, its impact rippling out from the United States, affecting nearly every country in the world, whether industrial producers or agricultural countries. The increased economic interdependence in the world heightened the problems and showed how the world economy was flawed. Industrial production increased in Europe during the 1920s, especially in traditional industries such as coal, steel and shipbuilding, at the expense of newer consumer industries. The United States developed the latter, particularly the motor car industry, and the American economic growth rate outstripped Europe's, leaving Britain, France and Germany with a relative decline in their share of world trade. Agricultural prices were falling under the impact of mechanization, so producers of raw materials had to reduce the quantity of imported manufactured goods to compensate. U.S. tariff barriers against European products had a harsh effect. Investments left Europe in search of higher interest rates elsewhere and the cycle of indebtedness established around German reparations payments merely confused matters further. American loans were made to Germany to help reparations payments to France and Britain, who could then repay interest to the U.S. for wartime loans. In this situation the Wall Street crash caused severe hardship, especially with the recall of U.S. European loans, damaging Germany in particular. Many industrial countries incurred 25 per cent unemployment rates (Germany 30.1 per cent, France 24.3 per cent, Austria 26.1 per cent, Denmark 31.7 per cent); industrial production fell to 53 per cent in Germany, and social distress was immense. In Germany malnutrition was rife, meat consumption fell and the death rate increased, while in England this despair is best exemplified by the hunger marches from the Jarrow shipyards to London. Government reactions to the Depression sometimes exacerbated the distress. Import tariffs were strictly applied all over Europe, and even Britain ended its eighty-six years of free trade by the 1932 Import Duties Act and the Ottowa Imperial Conference, which granted preferential treatment to Dominion agricultural products, while British manufactured goods received reciprocal treatment in Dominion markets. France adopted similar tactics regarding her own colonies. Additionally, European states adopted deflationary policies, especially in Germany and France; budgetary control in Britain; and government intervention in Nazi Germany, concentrating on promoting heavy industry and a public works programme. In Britain the revival of domestic consumer demand provided with cheap money helped private enterprise and gradually turned around the economy. The Depression had a significant impact on domestic and international politics. Democracies experienced unusual political tendencies. Ministerial crises in France and the development of Fascist leagues, the Croix de Feu, led in 1936 to Léon Blum's Popular Front government, a sister system to that in Spain. Britain ended the normal single-party government and switched to a multi-party national government in the face of international events and Mosley's British Union of Fascists. Support for right-wing extremist parties grew, from the Lapua movement in Finland to the Hungarian Arrow Cross. Ruined farming interests backed the right (Romania's League of the Archangel Michael) and many middle-class voters in Germany brought Hitler to power.

THE DEPRESSION

percentage of industrial workers
unemployed

- 31.7
- 28
- 23
- 18
- 13
- no data

- strike waves
- sit-down strikes
- riot, demonstration or single strike

Norwegian Sea

Arctic Circle

FINLAND

Helsinki
Tallinn
ESTONIA
Leningrad
Stockholm
Riga
LATVIA
LITHUANIA
Kaunas
Königsberg
Danzig
free city under
League of Nations
East Prussia
Warsaw
Brest Litovsk
U.S.S.R.

Oslo

North Sea

Glasgow • Edinburgh
UNITED
KINGDOM
DENMARK
Copenhagen
Hamburg
Berlin
POLAND

IRELAND
Liverpool
Hull
Bristol
Birmingham
London
Calais
Brussels
BELGIUM
Amsterdam
NETHERLANDS
Rhine
GERMANY
Frankfurt
Prague
Cracow
Lvov
CZECHOSLOVAKIA

*Faeroe Islands
to Denmark*

ATLANTIC OCEAN

SAAR
autonomous under
League of Nations
Paris
Orléans
FRANCE
Lyon
Bordeaux
Marseille

Bern
SWITZERLAND
AUSTRIA
Vienna
Budapest
HUNGARY
ROMANIA
Bucharest
R. Danube
Black Sea

Milan
Trieste
Genoa
Venice
YUGOSLAVIA
Belgrade

BULGARIA
Sofia

ANDORRA
Barcelona
Rome
ITALY
Naples
ALBANIA
Istanbul
TURKEY

Lisbon
PORTUGAL
Madrid
SPAIN
Alicante
Balearic Is.
GREECE
Aegean Sea
Izmir
Athens
Italian occupied

Cádiz
Gibraltar
to Great Britain
Almería
Tangier
international
zone
Mediterranean Sea

Morocco
Algeria
Tunisia
to France

Libya
to Italy

PART VIII: MODERN TIMES

A poster supporting the Hitler Youth, a march and rally to be held in Nuremberg, 1938.

All the states of continental Europe, with the exceptions of Sweden, Switzerland and Portugal, had been occupied, defeated, bombed, pillaged, fought over and liberated between 1939 and 1945; Spain was suffering from the effects of its civil war between 1936 and 1939. Europe had suffered; Europe had been broken, national institutions and infrastructures had been suppressed and wrecked and millions of European citizens had been thrown into prison, murdered or carried off into slavery. All, whether conquerors or conquered, underwent a terrible experience during these war years and with hindsight it might not seem unnatural that many intelligent citizens of European nation-states should have begun to nurse apparently heretical doubts about the continuing validity and sacrosanctness of the nation-state. It was such a mood that not only gave rise to the project of European integration, but also to the intellectual movements of existentialism and, in more recent times, post-modernism.

The first need was to rebuild Europe, first through the Marshall Plan, officially termed as the European Recovery Programme, then after 1950, through European-led initiatives. It was these initiatives that led to the establishment, in 1950, of the European Coal and Steel Community, which paved the way for the 1957 Treaty of Rome and the hopes, of some, for a federated Europe.

Without doubt the overriding issue confronting Europeans in the aftermath of the Second World War was the impact of the Cold War. The origins of the Cold War may be found in the Yalta Conference of February 1945, when the "Big Three" Allied powers, the United States, the Soviet Union and Great Britain, began to plan the peace that would follow the Second World War. Some commentators, including this writer, believe that with hindsight the Cold War can actually be pre-dated to the period of the Russian Civil War (1918–1921), during which Allied military intervention in Russian affairs led to deep-seated Soviet suspicions of the Western powers. Whatever the case, growing suspicions of Soviet intentions by the United States and Great Britain were fuelled by their inability to resolve satisfactorily disagreements between the Allied powers. As former allies ceased to be friends, the European continent fell subject to a bitter bipolar cleavage, based upon the ideological difference of two entirely different political, social and economic systems held between "East" and "West".

The Soviet Union and its satellites — Albania (until 1961), Bulgaria, Czechoslovakia, Eastern Germany, Hungary, Poland and Romania — were supported through the Zhdanov policy of 1948, which was the ideological and economic alternative to the rejected Marshall Aid and the Truman Doctrine. To a lesser extent this was bolstered by the ideological campaigns of Communist parties and their fellow travellers in Western Europe, where Communists in the first decade after the war were winning 25 per cent of the electorate in countries such as France and Italy. It cannot be denied that Communism had a strong appeal in some European states in the immediate post-war period and this was built upon the link between Communist parties with resistance movements after the German invasion of the Soviet Union in 1941. For example, in France the Communist Party was seen by many as being the *Parti des fusillés*, since 75,000 Communist "patriots" had been executed by the German occupiers between 1940 and 1945.

The Cold War was dominated by the interests of the two superpowers, whereby the United States aimed to contain the Soviet Union and the spread of Communism, while post-war Soviet leaders aimed to provide for the total security of their country; hardened as they were by the expenditure of tremendous efforts and vast population losses suffered during the First World War, the Civil War and the Second World War, or Great Patriotic War as the Soviets termed it. Europe was divided into two hostile blocs ranging along the "iron curtain", which cleaved Europe into two. Europe, especially the north German Plain, became one of the "front lines" of the East-West divide, where NATO forces confronted Warsaw Pact forces, without a shot being fired in anger. Western leaders were concerned with the threat of a Warsaw Pact Blitzkrieg-type attack, which might sweep rapidly through Germany to the North Sea coast. To counter this situation, nuclear weapons held the stalemate, since throughout the Cold War, in order to maintain peace, both sides believed in the strategies of deterrence and relied upon the existence of nuclear weapons in the face of protests against European governmental policies by peace movements in the early 1960s and 1980s.

Despite this the wishes and aspirations of the peoples of eastern Europe were not taken into account. During the slight thaw that followed the death of Stalin in March 1953, there was discontent in Poland and East Germany; then in 1956, revolution broke out in Hungary, where nationalist opinion was influenced by the recent granting of independence to Austria as a neutral state in 1955. Soviet forces invaded Hungary and the streets of Budapest were shelled by the Red Army. Some 190,000 Hungarians fled into exile while their leader, Imre Nagy, was executed. Hungary was soon forced back into the Soviet fold.

The period 1963–1978 witnessed a gradual détente, or relaxation, of East-West tensions, despite the Soviet invasion of Czechoslovakia in 1968, when Czechoslovaks had rallied to General Secretary Alexander Dubcek's (1927–1993) appeal to "socialism with a human face", expressing themselves in lively debate and criticism and demonstrating in the streets of their capital, in what was known as the short-lived Prague Spring, only to be crushed by Soviet tanks.

The Conference on Security and Co-operation in Europe, held at Helsinki in August 1975, accepted the need for developing economic relations and recognized the post-war frontiers of Europe. The mood of the conference was one of conciliation and détente. As part of Willy Brandt's Ostpolitik, the Federal Republic of Germany accepted the postwar frontier with Poland, and West Berlin was no longer interpreted as part of the Federal Republic.

By the 1960s, the Soviet Union had achieved parity with the United States in the military sector. This parity, however, led to a huge drain on Soviet resources. The Soviet Union's GNP was only half the size of that of the United States, yet it had to devote a far greater proportion of its resources to defence in order to compete. A two-track economy developed in the Soviet Union between military and consumer needs. In addition, ten years of warfare in Afghanistan proved a costly failure to the Soviet Union and ended in ignominious defeat in 1988–1989.

"Die breite Masse eines Volkes...einer grossen Lüge lieber zum Opfer fällt als einer kleinen."
"The broad mass of the nation...will more easily fall victim to a big lie than to a small one."
Adolf Hitler

The problems of a divided Europe are commented on in this German magazine of 1949: two peoples, two countries, two leaders.

Maintaining Soviet control over the economically weak Eastern European buffer zone was costing too much and producing little of any benefit. President Reagan's Strategic Defence Initiative (Star Wars) eventually constituted an even greater strain on the Soviet economy.

The Cold War had entered a second phase of deteriorating relations with Soviet intervention in Afghanistan; this was reinforced by the election of Ronald Reagan as U.S. president in 1980, with his invective against the "evil empire". Similarly the imposition of martial law in Poland in December 1981 led to a further deterioration of East-West relations which, with the shooting down of the Korean airliner, flight KAL 007, by Soviet fighter aircraft, resulted in what some commentators have termed as the "Second Cold War".

Because of the great importance attached to military security during the Cold War, other issues and events in international relations were considered to be of lesser importance, such as the project of European integration that stemmed from the Treaty of Rome in 1957, or the degree of communication between the two halves of Europe. These either played a subordinate role or were treated as security issues in themselves. From a United States point of view this often meant two conflicting attitudes toward European integration, either as a vital necessity to the cohesion of the West, particularly in support of the NATO alliance, or as a potential threat to both the economic and political leadership of the United States.

In the 1980s, the cost of the Afghan War and "Star Wars" rivalry were placing great strain upon the Soviet economy. The USSR was spending between 11 and 15 per cent of its GNP on defence in comparison with between 6 and 7 per cent in the United States. The gap between military and civilian economies demonstrated a need for greater dialogue with the West, and a series of reforms, known as *perestroika* and *glasnost*, advocated economic reform and greater transparency.

By the end of 1989, the once monolithic Soviet Communist Party was losing its political pre-eminence, against a background of popular dissatisfaction with the Soviet government and the rising problem of nationalism and inter-ethnic disputes. By the time of a failed coup of August 1991, it was clear that the Soviet Communist Party had lost its authority and that the Soviet Union was rapidly disintegrating. In December 1991, the Soviet Union ceased to exist, giving place to a loose alliance called the Commonwealth of Independent States. The political and social upheaval in the fifteen successor states to the former USSR constitutes one of the most momentous events affecting Europe in the latter part of the twentieth century.

After the end of the Cold War, the whole issue of European security and defence underwent tremendous transformation. Before the end of the Cold War, the threat of interstate conflict in western Europe had been almost unimaginable. But the experiences of former Yugoslavia and Chechnya have shown different, and the issues of nationalism and minority rights in eastern and central Europe have caused considerable concern. Since 1991, concerns have been expressed not so much over the possibility of interstate conflict, as that of intrastate conflict — a non-European as well as a European issue. In moments of pessimism, some influential European politicians even talked of "former" Yugoslavia as being a laboratory for the rest of Europe, although at the time of writing, the Yugoslav experience has been shown to be an exception rather than a norm. Likewise minorities' issues have soured relationships between the Hungarian, Romanian and Slovak governments over the 9 per cent Hungarian minorities living in both Slovakia and Hungary, or in the Baltic States of Latvia, Estonia and Lithuania, which have 30 per cent or more Russian minority populations. In the West, regional movements have asserted themselves in Spain since the transition period following the death of Franco in 1975 (Basques, Cataláns and Galicians), in Italy (Umberto Bossi's Northern League, which even tried to establish an independent Padania in September 1995) and in Belgium, where tensions between Walloon French speakers and the Flemish have consistently influenced Belgian politics since the 1950s. Oft-perceived regional and national differences are becoming more and more blurred. Whereas in the period 1989–1992 academics and political commentators argued that European integration was becoming a greater reality in contradistinction to the break-up of eastern and central European states, throughout the 1990s the idea of a Europe of the regions, with greater decentralization, has become the reality. In the mid-1990s, a sense of failure concerning European-led security projects led to reliance again upon the military and political weight of the United States in what had been described euphemistically as "Europe's backyard".

The conflicts in Bosnia-Herzegovina have also demonstrated a change in attitude to peacekeeping; since the Dayton Agreements of November 1995, peacekeeping based upon impartiality has been transformed into the more interventionist and proactive policy of peace enforcement, with the introduction into Bosnia of IFOR, then SFOR troops who work to keep the different factions apart.

Current developments on the European political scene gravitate around different issues, such as: the deepening and widening of the European Union; the impact of defence organizations, such as NATO in East Central Europe, upon the CIS, with the policy of "Partnership for Peace", which has caused great concern in Russia; minority and human rights issues and internal security issues with the policies of ending borders within the EU, the Schengen policy set against concerns expressed over the influx of economic and political migrants from East Central Europe; European initiatives in developing security and defence organizations, such as "Eurocorps", the European Community for Security and Co-operation (ECSC); and the Western European Union and the changing nature of Europe, whereby North-South divisions and tensions have replaced East-West tensions, resulting in growing tensions between richer and poorer states and societies. If Hungary, Poland, the Czech Republic and Slovenia are in the next round of negotiations for entry into Europe, one wonders what will happen in turn to some of the Balkan states, such as Albania, Bulgaria, Macedonia, Romania and Yugoslavia (Serbia and Montenegro). Will these states and peoples, which have played their role in the European mainstream across the centuries, now be excluded from the new European *imperium*, as their ancestors were one and a half millennia previously? Perhaps the biggest problem in Europe at the dawn of the new millennium is that of exclusion and identity.

THE FASCIST STATES

*A poster from 1938
celebrating the
Hitler-Mussolini Pact.*

"Fascism accepts
the individual
only insofar as
his interests
coincide with the
state's."
Benito Mussolini

The aftermath of the First World War with its peace treaties of Versailles, St. Germain, Neuilly and Trianon reconstructed much of Europe into a patchwork of new and economically unviable states. The resentment felt by the defeated powers and the failure to put President Wilson's principle of the self-determination of peoples into practice left ethnic minorities in virtually every country, creating irredenta all over Europe. The subsequent growth or resurgence of intense nationalism was further fuelled by inflation, the economic adjustment to peace.

The response to social, economic and political change and dislocation spawned protest movements throughout Europe; the weaker the democratic traditions and institutions, the more likely that a country would flirt with some form of right-wing political movements or parties. A further event colouring European political views was the apparent success of the Bolshevik Revolution in Russia, the consequent fear of the spread of Communism after the failure of socialist revolutions in Finland, some Baltic states, Germany, Hungary and Romania and the founding of the Soviet Comintern, probably reinforced the development of right-wing parties, especially those of the fascist variant.

The difficulties of the inter-war years were a fertile ground for fascism and its specific programmes to end national problems. Fascism sought to construct a society wherein the individual was subordinated to an organic state, where economic conflicts were reconciled in the corporate state and where duty and service to the state was accompanied by unquestioning loyalty to the leader, the *Führerprinzip*. Fascist regimes flourished between the wars, establishing themselves through the ballot box as in Germany and Italy, or by these countries' sponsoring or protecting such regimes in conquered or Allied states like Croatia, Slovakia and Albania.

Although fascist ideas developed before 1914, the concept of "action" derived from Sorel found a particular home in Benito Mussolini's Italy. The Italian dictatorship began in 1922, and despite his claims to be totalitarian, fascism never managed to permeate all aspects of society. Based on a leadership cult, Mussolini's Italy sought: domination over the Adriatic by backing the Fascist Croatian Ustashe and penetrating Albania economically; hegemony in the Mediterranean, with dreams of acquiring French Tunisia and Corsica; and extending her East African possessions into Abyssinia. The desire to rebuild a new Roman empire led to Italy's ruin in the Second World War.

The German variant of fascism, National Socialism, redolent of biopolitics, racialism, anti-Semitism and hostility toward democracy, was more brutal than its Italian forerunner. Successfully revising aspects of the Versailles Treaty, Hitler's foreign policy ambitions were grandiose — fantasies of a Central European empire in the search for *Lebensraum* and a central African imperium were part of a quest for world domination.

Both Hitler and Mussolini supported fascism elsewhere but other movements never achieved power except through Nazi or Italian support in the war. Even Germano-Italian support for Franco in the Spanish Civil War (1936–1939) failed to sway El Caudillo into a fascist stance: Franco remained a traditional, authoritarian, conservative, military leader, supported by the old Spanish elites.

THE FASCIST STATES

democratic countries

repressive or conservative countries

fascist countries

communist dictatorship

right-wing activity

200 km

200 miles

N

Arctic Circle

Norwegian Sea

Faeroe Islands
to Denmark

North Sea

Baltic Sea

NORWAY

SWEDEN

FINLAND

Oslo

Stockholm

Helsinki

Tallinn

Leningrad

ESTONIA

Riga

LATVIA

LITHUANIA

Kaunas

Königsberg

Danzig
free city under League of Nations

East Prussia

U.S.S.R.

Glasgow

Edinburgh

UNITED KINGDOM

Dublin

Liverpool

IRELAND

Birmingham

London

Amsterdam

NETHERLANDS

Brussels

BELGIUM

Calais

DENMARK

Copenhagen

Hamburg

Berlin

GERMANY

R. Rhine

Frankfurt

SAAR
autonomous under League of Nations

Warsaw

Brest Litovsk

POLAND

Cracow

Lvov

Prague

CZECHOSLOVAKIA

Vienna

Budapest

AUSTRIA

HUNGARY

ROMANIA

Paris

Orleans

FRANCE

Bern

SWITZERLAND

Lyon

Milan

Genoa

Trieste

Venice

Belgrade

YUGOSLAVIA

Bucharest

R. Danube

Bordeaux

ATLANTIC OCEAN

Marseille

ANDORRA

Barcelona

Madrid

SPAIN

PORTUGAL

Lisbon

Alicante

Cádiz

Gibraltar
to Great Britain

Almería

Tangier
international zone

Morocco

Balearic Is.

Rome

Naples

ITALY

Adriatic Sea

BULGARIA

Sofia

Istanbul

TURKEY

Izmir

ALBANIA

GREECE

Athens

Aegean Sea

Italian occupied

Black Sea

Mediterranean Sea

Algeria

Tunisia

to France

Libya
to Italy

141

WORLD WAR II, 1939–1942

THE AXIS EXPANSION, 1938–42

- Germany, 1939
- German invasion of Poland, 1938–39
- Soviet attack on Baltic states and Poland
- added to the Reich, 1936–40
- Axis satellites, 1939–44
- invasion of Denmark and Norway, April 1940
- Allied landing in Norway and withdrawal
- invasion of Netherlands, Belgium and France, May 10, 1940
- British attack on Libya from Egypt, 1940
- Western states conquered, 1940

- invasion of Yugoslavia and Greece, April 1941
- allied landing in Greece, withdrawal to Crete then Egypt, 1941
- Italian advance, 1941
- Eastern territories and Balkans conquered, 1941
- German support of Italy, campaigns to Egypt, Feb. 1941– Sept. 1942
- invasion of Russia, June 1941
- Soviet industrial plants move east, 1941–42
- conquered, 1942
- controlled by Vichy, 1942
- Allied controlled, late 1942
- neutral states

North Cape

Norwegian Sea

Arctic Circle

Narvik

Luleå

SWEDEN

NORWAY

FINLAND

Helsinki · Leningrad

Oslo

Stockholm

Baltic Sea

DENMARK

Copenhagen

Königsberg

East Prussia

SOVIET

Moscow

Dublin

IRELAND

UNITED KINGDOM

North Sea

Amsterdam

NETH.

Hamburg

Berlin

Warsaw

POLAND

Kiev

London

Brussels

BELGIUM

GERMANY

Frankfurt

Prague

CZECHO SLOVAKIA

Paris

Munich

Vienna

Aug. 1940 to Hungary

ATLANTIC OCEAN

FRANCE

Bern

SWITZ.

Geneva

AUSTRIA

Budapest

HUNGARY

ROMANIA

Vichy

11 Nov. 1942 occupied

Milan

Genoa

Venice

YUGOSLAVIA

Belgrade

R. Danube

Bucharest

B

Marseille

ITALY

Adriatic Sea

Sofia

BULGARIA

Istanbul

PORTUGAL

SPAIN

Corsica

Rome

Sardinia

ALBANIA

GREECE

Aegean Sea

TU

Lisbon

Madrid

Balearic Is.

Sicily

Athens

Crete

M e d i t e r r a n e a n   Sea

Algiers

Bone

Tunis

Malta to Britain

N

French North Africa

Tripoli

Benghazi

Lybia to Italy

E

Lybia to Italy

0   200 km
0   200 miles

The Second World War largely originated in the disputes and bitterness that had remained unresolved since the end of the First World War. The Germans were particularly bitter over the severe terms imposed upon them by the Treaty of Versailles.

By 1933, Adolf Hitler, leader of the extremely nationalist, anti-Semitic National Socialist Workers Party (NSDAP), was established in power and immediately began the rearmament of Germany. Benefiting from the reluctance of other European powers, especially Britain and France, to oppose him, he contravened the Versailles Treaty by sending German troops into the demilitarized Rhineland in March 1936. Later that year, Benito Mussolini, the fascist dictator of Italy, signed the Rome-Berlin "axis" agreement and the following year joined the Anti-Comintern Pact signed between Germany and Japan.

In March 1938, German forces occupied Austria, Hitler's birthplace, which was incorporated into the Third Reich (Anschluss). The following year the Germans, having incorporated the so-called Sudetenland by agreement in 1938, in turn annexed and neutralized what was left of Czechoslovakia.

On 1 September, 1939, Hitler having signed a non-aggression pact with the Soviet Union, German forces invaded Poland. Great Britain and France declared war on Germany two days later and on 16 September, Soviet forces invaded Poland from the east, dividing that country between the Third Reich and the Soviet Union. In the winter of 1939–1940, Estonia, Latvia and Lithuania, independent since 1918, were reoccupied by the Soviet Union, whose forces also invaded Finland and eventually occupied Karelia.

In April 1940, Germany occupied the whole of Denmark and several Norwegian ports and on 10 May, launched a Blitzkrieg (Lightning War) offensive in the west, sweeping through the Netherlands and Belgium into France. The bulk of the British Expeditionary Force, together with a large number of French troops, were evacuated at Dunkirk. An armistice was signed between Germany and France in June, with the Germans occupying Paris and the strategic northern and western seaboards of France, leaving central and southern parts to the control of Marshal Pétain's Vichy régime.

In August and September a bombing offensive, the Battle of Britain, was launched by Goering's Luftwaffe against the British, in an attempt to prepare the way for German troops to cross the English Channel and occupy Britain. However, the Royal Air Force won the day, forcing Hitler to break off his invasion plans.

In April 1941, Germany overran Yugoslavia and Greece; this diversion into the Balkans was in support of Hitler's Italian allies.

On 22 June, Hitler broke the Non-aggression Pact, caught the Red Army completely by surprise and drove deep into Soviet territory, overrunning Estonia, Latvia, Lithuania, Belorussia and Ukraine. However, he was eventually halted before Moscow and Leningrad by Soviet counter-attacks and resistance, aided by the long Russian winter.

In the summer of 1942, the Germans drove on toward the Black Sea and toward the Caucasus oilfields, only to be halted at Stalingrad and Ordzhonikidze, a Soviet victory that coincided with that of General Montgomery in El Alamein in Egypt. This was the high-water mark of the Axis advance.

WORLD WAR II, 1942–1945

THE AXIS COLLAPSE, 1942–45

→ Western Allies advance,
late 1942–Oct. 1943

⇢ German withdrawal

→ Soviet advance to Oct. 1943

→ Allied advance, 1943–45

→ German counterattack

◯ isolated German pocket

retaken by Allies,
Oct. 1942–Oct. 1943

retaken by Allies, Dec. 1944

retaken by Allies, end of
hostilities

still held by German armies,
9 May, 1945

When Japan attacked U.S. installations at Pearl Harbor, Hawaii, and the Philippines in December 1941, the United States declared war against all the Axis powers. Japan lost its initial advantage and momentum with the sea battles of the Coral Sea and Midway in the early summer of 1942.

Meanwhile, in North Africa British and Commonwealth forces who had been victorious against Italian opposition at the beginning of 1941 were now engaged in bitter fighting with Rommel's Afrika Korps with a campaign that swung back and forth across the western desert. Victory at El Alamein in November 1942 turned the tide of the desert war. That same month, U.S., British and Free French troops landed in North Africa and the Axis armies were forced out of North Africa into Sicily. By July, Allied troops landed in Sicily, invading Italy in September. The Italian fascist government signed an armistice with the Allies and in October the Italians declared war on Germany. Harsh fighting ensued with German forces that had moved into Italy. By the end of that summer, the Germans consolidated on the Gothic line, along the River Po, fighting throughout the autumn and winter of 1944.

In the meantime, the Red Army's victory over Von Paulus's Sixth Army at Stalingrad in February 1943 was followed in July by the greatest tank battle of the war at Kursk. The Red Army began to push the Germans back, so that throughout the winter of 1943–1944, the Red Army recovered much of occupied Soviet territory and in April 1944, advanced on Central Europe.

In June 1944, the Allies, under the supreme command of U.S. general Dwight Eisenhower, landed in Normandy, establishing a bridgehead in Europe and the much awaited Second Front. By 18 June, U.S. general Bradley had gained control of the Cotentin Peninsula, while British and Commonwealth forces took the city of Caen by 9 July, and advanced on Falaise, helping to surround the German Fifth and Seventh Armies; murderous aerial bombardments resulted in the deaths of some 60,000 German soldiers, thus momentarily breaking the spirit of German resistance. General Patton swept through France as Montgomery moved up the French coast. Paris was liberated by French general Leclerc on 26 August, and Brussels was liberated by British forces on 3 September.

Despite setbacks at Arnheim in the early autumn and the German counter-attack in the Ardennes during the bitter winter weather of December, the Rhine was crossed in February 1945, and the occupation of Germany began, as Soviet forces moved in from the east, occupying Berlin by the end of April. Hitler committed suicide on 30 April, and on 8 May, all German forces signed an unconditional surrender.

A German V-2 rocket is prepared for launching at a British target, beginning the ballistic missile age.

"Let us therefore brace ourselves to our duties, and so bear ourselves that, if the British empire and its Commonwealth last for a thousand years, men will still say; 'This was our finest hour.'"
Winston Churchill

RUIN, BANKRUPTCY AND RECOVERY

By 1945 many towns in Europe lay in ruins, such as Nuremberg, above. Only a massive injection of aid from the United States would hasten recovery.

It was a devastated Europe that emerged from the embers of the Second World War with its prestige in tatters throughout the world, but especially in the European colonies. Europe was economically and spiritually bankrupt, with transport, fuel, food and housing in short supply, to say nothing of the severe bomb and war damage, highlighted by the destruction of cities such as Berlin, Caen, Coventry, Dresden and London and many more. The ravages of war were compounded by a massive refugee problem of peoples returning to their homes in both the Soviet and Allied-controlled sectors.

Nevertheless, with the infrastructures of most European states destroyed, Europe had to rebuild itself. Before 1950, this project, at least in the West, was highly dependent upon American aid, especially Marshall Aid, officially known as the European Recovery Program (ERP), established in June 1947. The Soviet Union would refuse to accept Marshall Aid out of fear of American political, cultural and military hegemony. Consequently Eastern Europe, under Soviet influence, fell under the Zhdanov policy of 1948 with the concomitant internationalist and progressive Peace Movement and Comecon (Council for Mutual Economic Assistance) — a supranational economic agency, established in January 1949.

The ERP provided $6.8 billion in the first fifteen months of operation. Marshall Aid also created Inter Governmental Organizations (IGOs), which acted as agencies for European recovery and cooperation: the Organization for European Economic Cooperation (OEEC), which was made up of eighteen European countries, including the United States and Canada, provided $17,000 million between 1948 and 1952; the Technical Cooperation Administration (TCA) supplied technical and material support rather than financial aid.

The negative side of Marshall Aid was that it was seen by its detractors as being part of the apparatus of the Cold War. At the same time there were fears of Soviet influence, highlighted by large communist support at 25 per cent of the electorates of Italy and France. By the end of the 1940s, Europe would be split into two ideological blocs, "East" and "West"; two antithetical political, social and economic systems that lay at the heart of the Cold War scenario.

Concerns over external influence were felt within several European states, especially France, where a third force, neutralism, was advocated, proposing non-alignment with either Moscow or Washington; nevertheless this was poorly supported in the national elections of 1951.

The year 1950 proved to be a watershed in the process of European recovery, with the governments of several European states beginning to take greater control of their own affairs and destinies by demonstrating a serious intent toward economic and political collaboration. Recovery and reconstruction would provide the catalyst of the European project, based upon mutual cooperation, that would materialize with the Treaty of Rome in 1957.

The Marshall Plan greatly contributed to the recovery of Europe, restoring industrial and agricultural production and bolstering international trade. Marshall Aid allowed European states to modernize their economies and repair the dislocation of social patterns that had arisen from the Second World War.

"From Stettin in the Baltic to Trieste in the Adriatic, an iron curtain has descended across the Continent." *Winston Churchill*

POST-WAR EUROPE

→ displaced people, with number in thousand and dates

NATO member (1949–59)

Soviet bloc

Soviet sympathy

non-aligned

U.S. aid per country in millions of $ (Marshall Plan)

ICELAND

Norwegian Sea

Arctic Circle

NORWAY

SWEDEN

FINLAND

North Sea

DENMARK

IRELAND

UNITED KINGDOM

NETHERLANDS

ATLANTIC OCEAN

B.

G.F.R.

FRANCE

SWITZERLAND

Germans **8050** (1945–52)

Germans Berlin **1850** (1945–52)

G.D.R.

displaced persons (majority Jews) **960** (1947–51)

to U.K. America and South Africa

Germans **250** (1945–47)

Hungarians **200** (1946–47)

CZECHOSLOVAKIA

AUSTRIA

H.

Croats & Serbs **40** (1946)

Hungarians **40** (1946)

POLAND

Poles **3500** (1945–52)

Ukrainians **500** (1945–47)

U.S.S.R.

Poles **1500** (1945–46)

Germans **525** (1946–47)

Slovaks **60** (1946–47)

Slovaks **100** (1946–47)

ROMANIA

60 (1944)

Estonians **40** (1944–45)

50 (1944)

Latvians **100** (1944–45)

50 (1944)

Lithuanians **80** (1944–45)

Russians **2500** (1946–50)

Trieste free state

YUGOSLAVIA

BULGARIA

Black Sea

to Israel

Corsica

Sardinia

Germans **250** (1945–47)

Germans **300** (1945–48)

ITALY

ALBANIA

GREECE

Turks **160** (1950–52)

TURKEY

Aegean Sea

Crete

ANDORRA

PORTUGAL

SPAIN

Balearic Is.

Sicily

Gibraltar to Britain

Tangier international

to Spain

Morocco to France

Mediterranean Sea

ALGERIA to France

Tunisia to France

Malta to Britain

Libya to Italy

0 200 km
0 200 miles

400
200
0

147

EUROPEAN UNION

Not everyone was in favour of a new united Europe; a British political poster from the 1970s advocates withdrawal from the European Economic Union.

"The contribution which an organized and living Europe can bring to civilization is indispensable to the maintenance of peaceful relations."
Robert Schuman,
9 May, 1950

In the aftermath of the Second World War, the founding fathers of the project for European integration, among them Robert Schuman, Jean Monnet, Konrad Adenauer, Alcide de Gaspierri and Paul-Henri Spaak, sought to work together in a spirit of reconciliation to build Europe anew and to strengthen European economic competition in the world market place.

Although the European Economic Community was founded by the Treaties of Rome in March 1957, its origins lie in the Schuman Declaration of 9 May, 1950, which advocated the pooling together of coal and steel production, by establishing a single higher authority that would merge the coal, iron and steel industries of France, West Germany, Italy and the Benelux countries. The European Coal and Steel Community (ECSC) was also designed to be "a first step in the federation of Europe", in a bid to establish peace forever on the European continent by ending the traditional enmity between France and Germany. The ECSC began to function in July 1952 and would be merged with the EEC and Euratom in 1967, within the European Community.

A second significant development was the unsuccessful attempt to establish a European Defence Community among the six ECSC states. This project was launched by French Foreign Minister René Pleven and ratified by five of the member states in 1954, but rejected by the French Assemblée Nationale, due to a growing public opinion that was concerned with the rearmament of Germany.

In accordance with the Treaty of Rome, the European Community established common policies among the six member states for: agriculture, transport, the movement of capital and labour, and the erection of common external tariffs. A European Parliament was set up, meeting alternately in Strasbourg and Luxembourg, alongside the European Commission in Brussels and the European Court. Later the Lomé Conventions of 1975, 1979, 1984 and 1989 would establish development and technical cooperation aid programmes, and would ease customs duties for over sixty countries.

The United Kingdom, Ireland and Denmark joined the EEC in January 1973. The "nine" became ten when Greece followed in 1981 and then twelve in 1986, with the entry of Spain and Portugal. Sweden, Finland, and Austria became members of the European Union in January 1995.

A major development took place in 1992 with the signing of the Maastricht Treaty, which established the Single European Act. At its simplest level, this can be described as "an amendment of the Treaty of Rome plus citizenship", establishing a single European Act and a peoples' Europe based upon the three pillars of European security, the European Community and internal affairs.

As Europe enters the twenty-first century, two key issues, "deepening" and "widening", confront the European communities. To what extent does the Union progress further down the road toward becoming a federal, supranational state with, for example, its own army and a common European currency; and how does the European Union respond to the enormous changes that have taken place in Eastern Europe since the fall of the Berlin Wall in 1989 and the end of the Cold War?

EUROPEAN UNION

development of the European Community

- signature of the Treaty of Rome, 1957
- EEC member added 1973
- EEC member added 1981
- EEC member added 1986
- became part of the EEC after union of Germany, 1990
- EEC member added 1995
- membership pending, 1996

military alliances

- ● original member of North Atlantic Treaty Organization, 1949
- ○ later NATO member
- ★ Warsaw Pact, 1955–90
- △ neutral state

ICELAND

Norwegian Sea

FINLAND

Helsinki   Leningrad

Oslo

Stockholm   Tallinn
ESTONIA

Baltic Sea   Riga   LATVIA

LITHUANIA

Königsberg   Vilnius

RUSSIA

Gdańsk   (U.S.S.R.)
(until 1991)

North Sea

DENMARK
Copenhagen

Hamburg

Warsaw

Glasgow   Edinburgh

UNITED KINGDOM   Berlin   POLAND

Dublin   Liverpool   Amsterdam   GERMANY   Cracow   Lvov

IRELAND   Birmingham   The Hague   NETHERLANDS   (GERMAN FEDERAL REPUBLIC)   (GERMAN DEMOCRATIC REPUBLIC)

Bristol   Brussels   Frankfurt   Prague
London   BELGIUM   Rhine R.   CZECH   SLOVAKIA
Calais   1965   Bratislava

ATLANTIC OCEAN   Paris   Vienna   Budapest   ROMANIA

FRANCE   1966 withdrawal   Bern   AUSTRIA   HUNGARY

SWITZERLAND   Bucharest
Lyon   Trieste   Zagreb   R. Danube
SLOVENIA   Belgrade   Black Sea
Milan   Ljubljana
Bordeaux   Genoa   Venice   CROATIA   BOSNIA   SERBIA   BULGARIA
Marseille   Monaco   HERZEG.   Sarajevo   Sofia
ANDORRA   Sarajevo   Istanbul
ITALY   MONTE-NEGRO
Corsica   Rome   ALBANIA   Skopje
Barcelona   Tiranë   GREECE   Aegean   Izmir   1952
Madrid   Naples   1968 withdrawal   Sea
PORTUGAL   SPAIN   Sardinia   1952   Athens
1982   Alicante
Lisbon   Balearic Is.
Cádiz   Almería   Sicily
Gibraltar   Mediterranean   Crete
Tangier   to United Kingdom   Sea
CYPRUS
MOROCCO   ALGERIA   TUNISIA
LIBYA

0   200 km
0   200 miles

N

NEW HOPE, OLD DIVISIONS

NEW AND OLD STATES EMERGE, 1991–93

- reunited, 1990
- new state, 1991
- new state, 1992
- new state, 1993
- area not under control of new government
- ■ capital of new state

1. Serbian backed "Independent Krajina".

2. Serbian and Croatian populations seize control of their own ethnic areas.

3. Russian majority form Transnistrian Republic.

4. Gagauzian separatist movement.

5. Abkhazian separatist movement.

6. South Ossetian separatist movement.

7. Chechenian separatist movement.

8. Armenian population struggle to control Nagorno-Karabakh and adjacent territory to the south.

The fall of the Berlin Wall in November 1989 and the subsequent wave of change that swept through eastern Europe arose from a popular desire for liberalism and democracy nurtured by new hopes for a better standard of living and quality of life after forty-five years under the control of rigid, totalitarian Communist governments and their systems.

The early 1990s witnessed a difficult social and economic transition, which led to unemployment, where previously there had been over-manning or where technologies and industrial processes were considered to be behind those of the West; this coincided with cuts in welfare and social support and led to a new underprivileged class, whose sense of bitterness and feelings of exclusion and frustration was sometimes vented in sporadic outbursts of violence, tainted by nationalistic yearnings that hearkened back, in some cases, to deep-rooted dissatisfactions with settlements that had been established by the Paris Peace Conference of 1919–1920. Some historians saw in this a "rebirth of history" whereby the traditional bipolar and economic cleavage between East and West that had existed since the end of the Second World War had gone, replaced by older divisions and tensions such as ethnic nationalism, national and regional identity and religious difference.

With these developments there has been a rise in organized crime, black marketeering and mafia-related activities, particularly in some of the less economically advantaged east-central European states. Many commentators have also remarked upon the lack of a fully developed civil society, due to the former presence of a monolithic Communist party and earlier political and cultural differences from the West, which as this survey has shown, have existed since the end of the middle ages, if not since the fourth century. Since the time of the French Revolution these differences have often been expressed in terms of economic, social and political "backwardness" in the region.

In the 1990s outbursts of nationalism were experienced in both eastern and western Europe; with the rise of the NPD (National Democratic Party) in Germany and the MSI (Movimento Sociale Italiano) in Italy and regular returns of between 12 and 15 per cent for the Front National in the first rounds of successive French elections, or for the Vlaams Blok in the Flemish part of Belgium; nevertheless, nationalism has, by and large, remained a marginalized protest vote in the West.

In the East, by contrast, experience has been somewhat different. Extremes of ethnic nationalist violence were experienced in parts of the region after the breakup of the Soviet Union, particularly in Chechnya and also during the bitter wars of "former" Yugoslavia, most notably in Bosnia-Herzegovina and Croatia, with the attendant horrors of ethnic cleansing carried out by all factions. But Yugoslavia did not become the benchmark of nationalist difference for the rest of eastern and central Europe; indeed even among the Yugoslav successor states, Macedonia, Slovenia and Yugoslavia (Serbia and Montenegro) were spared the horrors of war and bitter interethnic conflict. Nevertheless the ordinary citizens of Serbia and Montenegro suffered considerably the economic effects of sanctions and hyperinflation prior to the signing of the Dayton Accords in November 1995.

Against this background concerns over the security of Europe in the aftermath of the Cold War have been placed high on the European agenda and one wonders if the announced withdrawal of SFOR troops from Bosnia-Herzegovina in June 1998 will lead to further outbreaks of conflict in southeast Europe, or whether the recent tensions in Albania and their potential implications upon Albania's neighbours: Montenegro, Serbia, Greece, Macedonia, Bulgaria and Turkey will transform the Balkans once again into a European "powder keg"?

Ethnic Diversity of Former Yugoslavia, c. 1990

- Slovenes
- Croatians
- Serbians
- Bosnian Muslims (Slavs converted to Islam after the Ottoman conquest)
- Macedonians
- Germans
- Italians
- Hungarians
- Romanians
- Albanians
- Turks
- Greeks

CHRONOLOGY

7000–6500 BC   Agriculture and cattle farming appear in the Aegean, begins spreading northward.

4000 BC   Metal smelting begins in the Balkans.

3000–2000 BC   First Cycladic civilization (Aegean). The use of bronze (copper and tin).

2000 BC   Minoan civilization (Crete). Trading begins throughout region.

1600 BC   Rise of Mycenaean civilization (Greece).

1550 BC   Stonehenge completed (Britain).

1300 BC   Fortification of Athens' acropolis.

800 BC   Rise of the Etruscans (northern Italy). Iron-working in Germany and Austria spreads westward.

750 BC   Formation of Greek city-states, throughout the Mediterranean. Rise of Athens and Sparta. Scythian horseman, from the Russian steppes, begin to spread into eastern Europe.

510 BC   Foundation of the Republic of Rome.

505 BC   Establishment of democracy in Athens.

500 BC   Germanic peoples expand through northern Europe.

490 BC   Greeks in Asia Minor rebel against Persian rule. Persians defeated by Athenians at battle of Marathon.

480 BC   Greeks defeat Persian invasion forces under Xerxes at the battles of Salamis, Plataea and Mycale. Greeks form the Delian League alliance.

450 BC   Celtic "La Tène" culture emerges in central Europe, spreads through northern Europe.

443 BC   Pericles elected to power in Athens.

431 BC   War begins between Athens and Sparta.

404 BC   Sparta victorious over Athens but then goes to war with Persia.

395 BC   Athenian coalition defeats Sparta.

390 BC   Gauls invade early Rome.

338 BC   Philip II of Macedon defeats the Greeks at the battle of Chaeronea.

334 BC   Philip's son Alexander defeats the Persians under Darius III and enters Egypt, founding Alexandria and his empire.

323 BC   Alexander's empire splits into "Hellenistic" kingdoms.

290 BC   Rome controls central Italy.

264–241 BC   First of three "Punic" (Phoenician) Wars between Rome and Carthage for control of the Mediterranean.

218–201 BC   Second Punic War. Carthaginian General Hannibal crosses the Alps and invades Italy from the north.

206 BC   The Romans conquer Spain.

149–146 BC   Third Punic War ends with the Romans razing Carthage and founding North African colonies. Macedonia and Greece fall under Roman control.

60 BC   Germanic and Celtic tribes attack central Gaul, prompting the campaigns of conquest by Julius Caesar.

46 BC   Julius Caesar becomes emperor after civil war in Rome.

31 BC   Octavian victorious at the battle of Actium, annexes Egypt, and becomes Emperor Augustus.

AD 43   The Romans invade Britain.

AD 70   Jewish revolt in Palestine; the Romans take Jerusalem. Christianity begins to spread through the eastern provinces.

AD 114   Roman empire at its height under Trajan.

AD 193   A year of six Roman emperors, assassinations and upheaval, resulting in civil war.

AD 195–217   Wars between the Romans and the Parthians, from Asia Minor.

AD 240–270   Encroachments on the empire by Goths, a Teutonic people from the River Vistula region. Eventually the Goths are driven back, but the empire is fragmenting.

AD 294   The empire reorganized and strengthened by Emperor Diocletian .

324   Constantine defeats his rival Licinius and reunites the empire, making Constantinople (formerly Byzantium) his new capital. Constantine declares Christianity the empire's official religion. Henceforth, the Roman emperors are all nominally Christian.

376   The Visigoths (western Goths) are driven by marauding Huns from central Asia across the River Danube and into the Roman Empire.

378   Romans defeated by the Visigoths at the battle of Adrianople.

395   The Roman empire is once again divided, between the two sons of Theodosius I. Visigoths invade Greece. Incursions from the north into Gaul and Spain by other Germanic tribes, the Vandals and the Suebi.

410   Rome sacked by the Visigoths under Alaric.

439   The Vandals capture Carthage; western Roman empire in collapse.

450   Germanic Angles, Saxons and Jutes invade Britain.

476   The German Odoacer proclaimed king of the western empire, usurping Romulus Augustulus.

486   Clovis founds Merovingian kingdom of the Franks in northern Gaul.

493   Ostrogoths (eastern Goths) seize power in Italy.

533   The Romans under Justinian regain control of Italy and North Africa.

600–1000   The eastern Byzantine Empire, based on Constantinople, grows steadily more powerful in Asia Minor and southeastern Europe, spreading Greek Orthodox Christianity and resisting Persian and Arab invasions. Slavs spread westward and southward.

650   Muslim Arabs begin attacking Byzantium.

680   Bulgars invade the Balkans, establishing a rival empire north of the Byzantine.

711   Muslims invade Spain from Morocco.

718   The Byzantines resist Arab siege of Constantinople.

732   Muslims defeated by Franks at the battle of Poitiers.

754   The foundation of the Carolingian dynasty.

774   Charlemagne invades northern Italy.

790   From Scandinavia, Viking and Danish raids begin on northern Europe, Britain and Ireland.

800   Charlemagne becomes emperor in Rome. Foundation of the Holy Roman (western) empire.

830   The Vikings reach Constantinople.

843   The Carolingian empire is divided by the Treaty of Verdun into areas roughly corresponding with modern France and Germany.

860–880   The Vikings seize Novgorod and Kiev, capital of Russia, and attack Constantinople.

890   Incursions begin into central and southern Europe by non-Christian Magyar horsemen from around the Danube (Hungary).

911   Vikings gain Normandy (northwestern France).

929   A Muslim caliphate is established at Córdoba (Spain).

955   The Magyars are defeated by German King Otto I at the battle of Lechfield (Augsburg).

959   England is unified under King Edgar.

960   Poland is unified by Miesko I.

962   Otto I is declared emperor in Rome.

983   The Slavs rebel against Germanic expansion eastwards.

1014   In Ireland, the Vikings are defeated by Munster King Brian Boru at the battle of Clontarf.

1018   The Byzantines gain control of Bulgaria.

1031   The caliphate at Córdoba is overthrown.

1066   The Norman invasion of Britain.

1071   The Normans invade Italy. The Seljuks decisively beat the Byzantines at the battle of Manzikert (Turkey).

1085   In Spain, Toledo is recaptured from the Muslims by King Alfonso I of Léon.

1095   The First Crusade is launched to liberate Palestine.

1125   The Germans expand eastward.

1147   The Second Crusade to Spain; Lisbon is recaptured.

1154   Angevin Henry II becomes king of England and France.

1170   Anglo-Normans seize Dublin (Ireland).

1204   The Franks conquer Byzantium in the Fourth Crusade.

1215   In England, King John's Magna Carta makes concessions to the barons.

1230   Mongol incursions into Russia begin.

1240   The Mongols invade Russia, Ukraine, Poland, Hungary and Bohemia.

1251   With the death of Frederick II, the Holy Roman empire collapses in Italy and Germany.

1261   Greek control of Constantinople is restored with coronation of Michael VIII.

1309   The Papacy is moved from Rome to Avignon (France).

1337   Start of the Hundred Years' War between France and England.

1378–1417   The Great Schism between rival papacies at Avignon and Rome.

1389   The Ottoman Turks gain control of the Balkans at the battle of Kosovo.

1418 Henry the Navigator launches Portuguese explorations of Africa.

1447 Gutenberg invents the printing press.

1453 The French recapture England's continental possessions. The Ottomans take Constantinople, bringing an end to the Byzantine empire.

1455–1485 The Wars of the Roses (Lancaster and York) in England.

1480 Ivan III, the first Russian tsar, overthrows the Mongols.

1492 The Granada emirate falls, ending Muslim rule in Spain. Columbus' landfall in the West Indies.

1494 Franco-Habsburg wars begin for control of central Europe.

1519 Charles V of Spain and Holland is elected Holy Roman emperor. Magellan circumnavigates globe.

1521 The Protestant Reformation

1532 English king Henry VIII breaks away from Rome; establishment of the Church of England.

1545 Counter-Reformation discipline instituted by the Roman Catholic Church at the Council of Trent.

1556 Ivan IV of Russia invades Volga basin.

1560–1598 Religious wars in France.

1559 The Dutch, aided by the English, rebel against Philip II of Spain.

1588 The Spanish Armada invasion force is defeated by the English.

1609 Dutch Republic gains independence.

1618–1648 Thirty Years' War between the Catholic and Protestant powers. Ends with the Treaty of Westphalia.

1642–1646 English civil wars result in the execution of the king.

1654 Ukraine ceded by Poland to Russia.

1660 The Restoration of the English monarchy under Charles II.

1661 Louis XIV accedes to French throne, initiating French expansion.

1683 The Ottomans besiege Vienna.

1699 Hungary ceded by the Ottomans to the Habsburgs.

1700 The Great Northern War begins between Sweden and Russia.

1702 The War of Spanish succession begins. England allies with Holland and Austria to stifle Louis XIV's ambitions.

1707 England and Scotland unite.

1709 The Swedes are defeated by the Russians under Peter the Great at the battle of Poltava.

1713 The War of Spanish succession ends with the Treaty of Utrecht .

1740–1748 The War of Austrian succession. England supports Maria Theresa against France, Spain and Prussia. Prussia annexes Silesia.

1756–1763 The Seven Years' War. England and Prussia fight France, Spain and Austria.

1776–1783 The American War of Independence from Britain ends with Treaty of Versailles.

1783 Russia annexes the Crimea.

1789–1802 The French Revolution.

1791 Russia captures Black Sea steppes from Turks.

1795 Partition of Poland.

1804 Napoleon becomes emperor of France .

1805 French and Spanish navy defeated by British at Trafalgar.

1805–1812 Napoleonic defeats of Austrians and conquest of Prussia, Italy and Spain. Napoleon invades Russia.

1815 Napoleon finally defeated by the British at Waterloo (Belgium). Congress of Vienna.

1821 Greek war of independence.

1845 Great Famine in Ireland starts heavy emigration to U.S.A.

1848 'The Year of Revolutions'; violent suppression widespread.

1852 The French republic falls; Napoleon III declared emperor.

1854–1856 The Crimean War.

1859 War between France and Austria over Lombardy.

1861, 1862 Italy and Romania proclaimed kingdoms.

1864 Russia stifles rebellion in Poland.

1866 Prussia annexes Schleswig-Holstein from Denmark, threatens Austria.

1867 Austro-Hungarian alliance forms with dual monarchy.

1870 Italian troops expel French from Rome.

1871 Prussia annexes Alsace and Lorraine from French, forms unified German empire. Establishment of the third French republic.

1878 The Treaty of Berlin; Bulgaria, Romania, Serbia and Montenegro become independent states.

1879 German alliance with Austro-Hungarians. Expansion of German navy.

1894 French alliance with Russians.

1904 French Entente Cordiale with Britain.

1905 The first phase of the Russian Revolution. The Tsar suppresses the revolt but grants civil liberties. Norway gains independence from Sweden.

1907 British entente with Russia.

1908 Austria annexes Bosnia and Herzegovina.

1912–1913 War in the Balkans.

1914–1918 The First World War.

1917 The Tsar abdicates, Bolshevik takeover in Russia. America enters War.

1918 Tide turns against the Germans, who sue for peace.

1919 Treaty of Versailles dismantles Austro-Hungarian empire, leaves Germany reduced, indebted and stripped of colonies. The League of Nations founded.

1922 Union of Soviet Socialist Republics (USSR) established by Lenin. Fascists under Mussolini gain power in Italy. In Ireland, 26 southern counties win independence (Eire), 6 northern counties (Ulster) remain British.

1923 French occupation of the German Ruhr.

1931 Spain declared a republic.

1933 Hitler becomes German chancellor; Nazis seize power, start re-arming.

1936 German occupation of the Rhineland. In Spain, General Franco seizes power, overthrowing the republic; civil war begins. In Russia, Stalin embarks on "Great Purges".

1938 Germany annexes Austria. Munich conference. Germany occupies the Sudetenland (Czechoslovakia). The Nazis initiate violent persecution of Jews.

1939 German-Russian non-aggression pact. Franco victorious in Spain. Second World War.

1945 United Nations established. The "Cold War" begins.

1947 Americans' Marshall Plan for economic reconstruction of Europe.

1947–1949 Greek civil war.

1948 Communist regimes installed in Czechoslovakia and Hungary. The Berlin airlift.

1949 North Atlantic Treaty Organization (NATO) founded.

1955 Warsaw Pact (Eastern Bloc treaty) instituted.

1956 Russians crush revolts in Poland and Hungary.

1957 European Economic Community (EEC) founded by the Treaty of Rome.

1959 Britain and non-EEC states form the European Free Trade Area (EFTA).

1961 East Germans erect the Berlin Wall. Russian Gargarin the first man in Space.

1962 Crisis over Russian attempt to station nuclear missiles in Cuba.

1968 "Prague Spring" in Czechoslovakia crushed by Russian troops.

1969 British troops sent into Northern Ireland; start of "the troubles".

1972 USSR signs SALT I arms limitation treaty with USA.

1974 Turks invade and occupy half Cyprus.

1975 Democracy restored in Spain.

1979 USSR invades Afghanistan. SALT II arms limitation treaty between USSR and USA, but not formally ratified.

1983 Beginning of Strategic Arms Reduction Talks (START) between USSR and USA.

1985 Gorbachev becomes reformist leader of USSR, introduces "Glasnost" and "Perestroika".

1989 Fall of Berlin Wall. Uprising in Romania.

1990 Reunification of Germany.

1991 Formal dissolution of USSR and Warsaw Pact, establishment of CIS (Russian Federation).

1992 EU recognizes former Yugoslav republics of Croatia, Slovenia and Bosnia-Herzegovina. Civil war in Bosnia. Denmark votes against membership in EU.

1995 Czechoslovakia splits into the Czech Republic and Slovakia. Dayton Accord brings NATO-enforced peace in Bosnia.

1997 Negotiations underway for admission to EU of Norway, Slovenia, Poland, Hungary and Czech Republic.

SELECT BIBLIOGRAPHY

The authors readily acknowledge the work of many scholars and works in publication which have been consulted in the preparation of this atlas.

Many remain in publication and can be recommended for further reading on the topics covered in this atlas. Among this selected bibliography are the following:

Anderson, M. S., *The Eastern Question*, Macmillan, 1966

Angold, Michael, *The Byzantine Empire, 1025-1204*, Addison Wesley Longman, 1997

Asch, Ronald G. *The Thirty Years' War, The Holy Roman Empire and Europe 1616-1648*, Macmillan, 1996

Ball, Simon, *The Cold War, An International History 1947-1991*, Arnold, 1997

Bell, P. M. H., *The Origins of the Second World War in Europe*, Longman, 1986

Bennett, Martyn, *The English Civil War*, Addison Wesley Longman, 1995

Boxer, C. R., *The Dutch Seaborne Empire 1600-1800*, Penguin, 1965

Bradford, Alfred S. (ed), *Philip II of Macedon*, Praeger, 1992

Bradley, Richard, *Rock Art and the Prehistory of Atlantic Europe*, Routledge, 1997

Bremner, Ian and Taras, Ray, *New States, New Politics: Building the Post-Soviet Nations*, Cambridge University Press, 1996

Brown, P., *The World of Late Antiquity*, Thames and Hudson, 1971

Browne, H., *Spain's Civil War*, Addison Wesley Longman, 1996

Bury, J. B., *A History of Greece*, Macmillan, 1977

Cain, P. J., and Hopkins, A. G., *British Imperialism, Crisis and Deconstruction 1914-1990*, Longman, 1993

Cain, P. J., and Hopkins, A. G., *British Imperialism, Innovation and Expansion 1688-1914*, Longman 1993

Calvocoressi, Peter, *Resilient Europe, 1870-2000*, Longman, 1991

Cameron, A., *The Later Roman Empire*, Fontana, 1993

Cameron, Euan, *The European Reformation*, Clarendon Press, 1991

Cawkwell, George, *Thucydides and the Peloponnesian War*, Routledge, 1997,

Coppa, F. J., *The Origins of the Italian Wars of Independence*, Addison Wesley Longman, 1992

Cottrell, Leonard, *Hanibal: Enemy of Rome*, Da Capa Press, 1992

Cunliffe, Barry, *The Ancient Celts*, Oxford University Press, 1997

David, Jean-Michel, *The Roman Conquest of Italy* Blackwell, 1996

Davies, J. K., *Democracy and Classical Greece*, Harper Collins, 1993

Davis, R. H. C., *A History of Medieval Europe from Constantine to Saint Louis*, Longman, 1988

De Blois, *An Introduction to the Ancient World*, Routledge, 1997

Dolukhanov, Pavel M., *The Early Slavs, Eastern Europe from the Initial Settlement to the Kievan Rus*, Addison Wesley Longman, 1996

Elton, G. R., *Reformation Europe*, Fontana, 1963

Esdaile, Charles J., *The Wars of Napoleon*, Addison Wesley Longman, 1995

Fisher, D. J. V., *The Anglo-Saxon Age, c. 400-1042*, Addison Wesley Longman, 1976

Freeman, Charles, *Egypt, Greece and Rome: Civilisations of the Ancient Mediterranean*, Oxford University Press, 1996

Furet, Francois, *The French Revolution, 1770-1814*, Blackwell, 1996

Gates, David, *Napoleonic Wars*, Arnold, 1997

Green, Miranda J., *The Celtic World*, Routledge, 1996

Grey, Ian, *Ivan III and the Unification of Russia*, Penguin, 1972

Hale, J. R., *Renaissance Europe, 1480-1520*, Fontana, 1971

Higgins, R. A., *Minoan and Mycenaean Art*, Thames and Hudson, 1967

Hosking, G., *A History of the Soviet Union*, Fontana, 1985

Huizinga, J., *The Waning of the Middle Ages*, London, 1924

Joll, James, *Europe since 1870, An International History*, Penguin, 1990

Jones, Martin, *The Counter Reformation*, Cambridge University Press, 1995

Judt, T., *A Grand Illusion, an Essay on Europe*, Penguin, 1997

Kennedy, Hugh, *Muslim Spain and Portugal*, Longman, 1997

Kershaw, Ian, *The Nazi Dictatorship, Problems and Perspectives of Interpretation*, Arnold, 1993

Kindleberger, Charles P., *The World in Depression, 1929-1939*, Allen Lane, 1973

Kirby, D., *Northern Europe in the Early Modern Period. The Baltic World 1492-1772*, Addison Wesley Longman, 1990

Klinchevskii, V. O., *A History of Russia*, Russell and Russell, 1960, 5 vols

Koenigsberger, H. and Mosse, G., *Europe in the Sixteenth Century*, Longman, 1968

Kunte, Martin (ed), *Suleyman the Magnificent and his Age*, Addison Wesley Longman, 1995

Lewis, G., *The French Revolution, Rethinking the Debate*, Routledge, 1993

Lewis, Paul G., *Central Europe since 1945*, Addison Wesley Longman, 1994

Macfie, A. L., *The Eastern Question, 1774-1923*, Longman, 1989

McAuley, M., *Societ Politics, 1917-1991*, Oxford University Press, 1992

McCauley, M., *The Soviet Union since 1917*, Longman, 1981

McGregor, Malcolm F., *The Athenians and their Empire*, UCL Press, 1991

Martel, G., *The Origins of the First World War*, Addison Wesley Longman, 1996

Martin, Janet, *Medieval Russia, 980-1584*, Cambridge University Press, 1995

Mason, John, *The Dissolution of the Austro-Hungarian Empire 1867-1918*, Longman, 1997

Megarry, Tim, *Society in Prehistory, The Origins of Human Culture*, Macmillan, 1995

Mellars, P., *The Neanderthal Legacy. An Archaeological Perspective from Western Europe*, Princeton University Press, 1996

Mitchell, Lynette G. and Rhodes, P. J., *The Development of the Polis in Ancient Greece*, Routledge, 1997

Moorhead, John, *Justinian*, Addison Wesley Longman, 1994

Niewyk, D. L., *The Holocaust: Problems and Perspectives*, Houghton Mifflin, 1997

Oakley, Stewart P., *War and Peace in the Baltic, 1560-1790*, Routledge, 1992

Okey, R., *Eastern Europe, 1740-1985, Feudalism to Communism*, Routledge, 1992

Ostrogorsky, G., *History of the Byzantine State*, Blackwell, 1968

Outram, Dorinda, *The Enlightenment*, Cambridge University Press, 1995

Parker, Geoffrey, *Europe in Crisis, 1598-1648*, Fontana, 1979

Parker, Geoffrey, *Spain and the Netherlands, 1559-1659*, Fontana, 1979

Payne, Stanley, *A History of Fascism*, University of Wisconsin Press, 1996

Polisensky, J. V., *The Thirty Years' War*, NEL, 1974

Porter, A. H., *European Imperialism*, Macmillan, 1994

Rankin, David, *Celts in the Classical World*, Routledge, 1996

Riasanovsky, N. V., *A History of Russia*, Oxford, 1984

Roberts, Michael, *Gustavus Adolphus*, Addison Wesley Longman, 1997

Runciman, Steven, *A History of the Crusades*, Cambridge University Press, 1951-54, 3 vols

Runciman, Steven, *The Fall of Constantinople, 1453*, Cambridge University Press, 1965

Sawyer, Peter (ed), *The Oxford Illustrated History of the Vikings*, Oxford University Press, 1997

Scharma, S., *Citizens, A Chronicle of the French Revolution*, Penguin, 1898

Schlieder, Theodor, *Frederick the Great*, Addison Wesley Longman, 1997

Service, R., *The Russian Revolution, 1900-1927*, Macmillan, 1986

Smith, Christopher, *Late Stone Age Hunters of the British Isles*, Routledge, 1992

Sonnino, Paul, *Louis XIV and the Origins of the Dutch War*, Cambridge University Press, 1989

Steinberg, S. H., *The Thirty Years' War and the Conflict for European Hegemony*, Edward Arnold, 1966

Stone, Norman, *Europe Transformed, 1878-1919*, Fontana, 1983

Stoneman, Richard, *Alexander the Great*, Routledge, 1997

Sutherland, D. M. G., *France, 1789-1815, Revolution and Counter-revolution*, Fontana, 1985

Taylor, A. J. P., *The Habsburg Monarchy*, Penguin, 1948

Thorpe, I. J., *The Origins of Agriculture in Europe*, Routledge, 1996

Urwin, D. W., *The Community of Europe, A History of European Integration since 1945*, Longman, 1994

Vernadsky, G., *A History of Russia*, Yale University Press, 1961

Vernadsky, G. A., *The Mongols and Russia*, Yale University Press, 1953

Waley, D., *Later Medieval Europe, From Saint Louis to Luther*, Longman, 1985

Wallace-Hadrill, J. M., *The Barbarian West, 400-1000*, Blackwell, 1996

Wedgewood, C. V., *The King's War 1641-1647*, Collins, 1958

Wedgewood, C. V., *The Thirty Years' War*, Penguin, 1957

Wegs, R., *Europe since 1945, A Concise History*, Macmillan, 1996

Wehler, Hans-Ulrich, *The German Empire 1871-1918*, Berg, 1985

Wells, Colin, *The Roman Empire*, Fontana, 1992

White, Steven, *After Gorbachev*, Cambridge University Press, 1993

Whittow, Mark, *The Making of Orthodox Byzantium, 600-1025*, Macmillan, 1996

Yapp, M. E., *The Near East since the First World War*, Longman, 1991

Index

ACKNOWLEDGMENTS

Pictures are reproduced by permission of, or have been provided by the following:

Bibliothèque Historique de la Ville de Paris: p. 47.
e.t. archive: pp. 12, 13, 20, 22, 24, 29, 31, 32, 36, 38, 40, 42, 48, 50, 57, 58, 60, 62, 66, 72, 77, 87, 88, 90, 96, 98, 100, 102, 104, 108, 118, 125, 128, 131, 136, 138, 140, 146, 148.
Gibert, Elsa: p. 51.
Hulton Deutsch Picture Library: pp. 115, 134.
Image Bank: p. 124.
Imperial War Museum: p. 145.
Lauros-Girandon: p. 110.
Metropolitan Museum of Art: p. 55.
Novosty, London: p. 95, 116.
Peter Newark's Historic Pictures: p. 83.
Private Collections: pp. 10, 18, 44, 114.

Illustrations: Peter A. B. Smith

Design: Malcolm Swanston

Typesetting: Shirley Ellis, Marion M. Storz

Cartography: Peter Gamble, Elsa Gibert, Peter A. B. Smith, Malcolm Swanston, Isabelle Verpaux, Jonathan Young

Production: Marion M. Storz

Printing: Kyodo Printing Singapore Pte Ltd.